MIGRANT STUDENTS MATTER

Stories of Triumph and Approaches That Work

MIGRANT
STUDENTS
Matter

STORIES OF TRIUMPH AND
APPROACHES THAT WORK

Dr. Paul Cade

Anomar Press
Immokalee, Florida

Migrant Students Matter:
Stories of Triumph and Approaches That Work

Copyright © 2024 Pete Cade

Published by Anomar Press
1240 Friendship Way
Immokalee, FL 34142

The author may be contacted by email at petec90@gmail.com

Cover and Interior Design by Imagine! Studios
www.ArtsImagine.com

Cover Images: Mykola Mazuryk/stock.adobe.com,
jongjawi/stock.adobe.com

ISBN: 979-8-218-38449-4

Library of Congress Control Number: 2024904138

First Anomar Press printing: March 2024

To my first teacher, my mom.

Your resilience and tenacity shaped me to be who I am today. You are missed daily, but are forever in my heart.

Table of Contents

Preface: Migrant Students Matter ix

Chapter One
Introduction: The Migrant Defined 1

Chapter Two
Roadblocks Along the Migrant Route 13

Chapter Three
Let's Take Attendance: From Migrant to Magnificent 27

Chapter Four
The Teachers that Mattered: Impactful and Integral 49

Chapter Five
Theme One: The Need to Understand the Migrant
Student Lifestyle 57

Chapter Six
Theme Two: Individualized and Supplemental
Instruction Works to Close Learning Gaps 63

Chapter Seven
Theme Three: Experiences that Motivate Gains and
Celebrate Milestones are Essential to Success 73

Chapter Eight
Theme Four: Using ALL Resources Available,
Including Parent Involvement, is Key! 81

Chapter Nine
A Summary of the Themes: A Bundle for Success 91

Chapter Ten
Connections to the Research 103

Chapter Eleven
The Migrant Author: Connections to Self, Every
Migrant Mile of the Way 109

Chapter Twelve
Conclusion 115

References 121
About the Author 137

Preface:
Migrant Students Matter

From the monarch butterfly to the humpback whale, migration is hardly ever voluntary. The need to move seasonally in order to find better living conditions and food, no doubt, requires a level of realization and adaptability. For the migrant family, the reasons and requisites are no different. When farmworker families have to migrate, however, for reasons far beyond their control, the effects are multifaceted with an array of factors that must be considered. Being displaced as a result of crop rotations that cut production and halt the work force, puts these families in positions where relocation is inevitable.

Understandably, the issue is amplified when children are involved. Moving from school to school and often times from state to state, can be taxing and unsettling. Differentiation in community cultures and misaligned education standards are enough to conjure up fear and unease. Coping with change is never easy. For the migrant students, many who have limited English proficiency and impending learning gaps, the efforts to help them succeed are overwhelming.

Within the pages that follow, the educational recommendations from former migrant students are presented. Questioned about their experiences in school, the now college graduates provide a keen insight into what they feel worked, supported their needs, and kept them working towards furthering their education. Simultaneously, they indicate, without reservation, what they saw as critical hindrances, negative encounters with assumed support, and far-fetched expectations. With a clear awareness that the graduation rate for migrant students is in need of refinement, their contributions towards how to best support the future of migrant education is both distinctive and essential.

Coupled with migrant student endorsements of best practices were responses from some of their favorite and most esteemed former teachers. As the former migrant students spoke about their experiences, they were eager to give accolades to their most valuable cheerleaders. The teachers who became more than just presenters of concepts and skills, seen to them as lifesaving agents, were also asked to participate in this study, in which the main objective was to compose a list of dos and don'ts when providing educational support to a unique group of students. Their corroboration of student positions adds another important layer to the solidification of a scrupulous assemblage of what works best when educating migrant students.

Bound in inquiry and supported by research, the narrative at hand takes a closer look at what today's teachers of migrant students need to know. Former migrant students who each went on to earn their respective college degree, backed by some of their most influential educators can't all be misguided. While some of their points to ponder may appear obvious at first glance, it is only when they are practiced with fidelity and in combination with their other submissions that best results will be yielded.

Chapter One

Introduction: The Migrant Defined

ince the 1990s, survey numbers have cited immigrants as making up 5% of the United States population. The figures more than doubled to 11% by the early 2000s. Statistics from 2014 indicated that U.S. migrant population was 13%. Most recent numbers, skewed by unconfirmed illegitimate entries have numbers closer to the 16–18% range. Regardless of the open-borders debate side that one is on, the reality of a booming migrant student population is here. As migrants enter the United States, illicitly or not, their limited English skills lead many to agricultural farm work that follows the crop seasons across the country. Most migrant children live below the poverty line, with incomes of less than $10,000 annually. The erratic enrollments of migrant students into our schools makes it difficult to pinpoint specific practices to best support them academically. A large-scale study conducted by the U.S. Department of Education found that principals and teachers held these students to low expectations, which mirrored the students' poor performance.

Established by the U.S. DOE in 1966, the Migrant Education program has spearheaded efforts to meet the educational and social needs of the unique migrant student population. There was a clear understanding that as a result of the students' experiences and lack of stability, they needed extra support and attention to be successful in the classroom. Furthermore, these students arrive on unfamiliar campuses where their cultural differences forfend assimilation and attract discrimination and xenophobia. When these students begin to see themselves as outcasts and in the midst of an obvious achievement gap, some students decide to drop out of school. Determining protocols to help migrant students avoid such adversities and best approaches to their learning are vital to the success of migrant education.

By criteria defined by the U.S. DOE, a migratory child is a child (ages 3–21) who (a) is a migratory agricultural worker or a migratory fisher; or (b) has moved within the preceding 36 months, in order to accompany or join a parent, spouse, or guardian who is a migratory agricultural worker or a migratory fisher who (i) has moved from one school district to another; (ii) in a state that is comprised of a single school district, has moved from one administrative area to another within such district; or (iii) as the child of migratory fisher, resides in a school district of more than 15,000 square miles, and migrates a distance of 20 miles or more to a temporary residence. The most recent data from the U.S. Department of Education for the 2020–21 school year illustrated that in 49 states, migrant education programs have served a total of

178,125 students in preschool through 12th grade, including an additional 14,714 out of school youth. (U.S. DOE, 2017).

The lifestyle of traditional migrant students creates barriers and inequalities in their learning. Constantly changing schools, enrolling late and withdrawing early, and being unable to speak English all work against them in their educational endeavors, stifling their goals of being gainfully employed contributors to their communities. The struggle to adjusting culturally and connect with peers and educators has created a need to repeal and validate the common practices currently in place. Irizarry and Williams (2013) argued that the academic and interpersonal struggles of migrant students stem from their families' lack of trust in the U.S. educational system. In examining what both migrant students and teachers of migrant students see as inevitable to their success, it is possible to isolate a set of systems, models, and mindsets to best teach this exclusive student population.

The 2020 U.S. Census Bureau report identified Hispanics as the largest ethnic group in the United States, with children enrolled in public schools who speak languages other than English. Approximately 80% of migrant students come from a Hispanic background, and one third of these migrant students have been born outside of the United States with Mexicans being the largest subgroup of English language learners (ELLs) in America's schools.

As this unique migrant population travels the country in search of agricultural work, the length of migrants' temporary residence depends on the particular crop and its harvesting window, and the stay can be interrupted by changes in weather. The ill-effects of migrant circumstances include the challenges of educational success. Insufficient resources and personnel can cause migrant students to be placed into inappropriate courses that reduce their actual potential for success. Concurrently, the same language challenges intensify alienation and prejudgments that cause them to feel oppressed.

Migrant parents themselves often are unable to advocate for their children, as they are unaware or ill-advised of how the public education system operates or their children's right to education. The value of parental involvement in public education has been firmly established as an important component of the academic success of all children, yet few studies have examined this construct from the frame of reference of migrant parents who are often marginalized by the educational system. Keeping records from each school transfer makes the process difficult, taking students away from being educated. In sum, migrant students are at a disadvantage and their road to success is fraught with challenges.

Migrant workers of all backgrounds and ethnic groups share common experiences and struggles, including poverty and racism. This analysis, however, is centered on Mexican-American migrants, who make up the majority student population in the United States. Migration by Mexicans into the United States originated with mass deportations that occurred prior to the Mexican War, when Mexico's economy collapsed forcing many families north. Their migration was essential to their survival, and their journey is a dangerous one. In current news, their struggles to enter the United States legally or not still remain.

A majority of migrant students across the country struggle to achieve educational success because of the problem of developing and providing best practices in migrant education. Téllez and Varghese (2013) explained that most education experts have ignored the education of language learners and the professional development of bilingual educators while simultaneously advocating for multicultural education. Additionally, migrant students who are instructed in their home countries arrive in the United States with varying knowledge, skill, and strategies for approaching and solving problems (Schleiler, 2015). The lack of multicultural education focused on bringing about educational equality continues to be a barrier for minority students (Banks, 2010).

Despite migrant student success stories, they are limited in comparison to those who fail. But from these success stories best practices for all migrant students can be developed. In 2012, the American Psychological Association (as cited in Vega, Lasser, & Plotts, 2015) identified an array of challenges that require those involved in their education, including administrators and teachers, be prepared to manage. Appropriate assessment and placement, mental health needs, and socio-emotional impacts of discrimination must be understood by educators to provide proper services (Vega et al., 2015). Stemming from relocation, language barriers, and cultural differences, the problem with inequalities between migrant students and their non-migrant counterparts must be examined to effect a reversal of its outcomes.

Learning the English language is required for success in American schools and is not easy. Moving from school to school at irregular intervals adds to the difficulty, and district services and programs provided vary. English language proficiency is an obstacle for many immigrant children. Early proficiency in the language is a crucial factor, closely related to positive academic achievement and graduation (Tavassolie, Lopez, DeFeyer, Hartman, & Winsler, 2018). On the 2017 National Assessment of Educational Progress, ELLs in fourth grade scored 40 points below non-ELLs in reading. ELLs at the eighth-grade level saw ever greater gaps at 47 points in reading (Nation's Report Card, 2018). The proficiency gaps varied from state to state; however, the need to make universal improvements is evident. Inevitably, there are differences in how each school district serves their migrant and ELLs. Establishing consistent approaches and levels of support could systematically take a defective system and turn it into one that is aligned with methodologies with proven results.

Issues for migrant students continue to grow as accountability through high-stakes testing becomes more prominent. This practice in itself has isolated undocumented migrant students who are not proficient enough to complete the assessments successfully (Green, 2003). As a general practice, these critical assessments are administered strictly in English (Contreras, 2011). Unfortunately, migrant students predominantly attend schools where teachers are less experienced with preparing their students for annual standardized assessments (Contreras, 2011).

Schools have a critical role to play in the settlement of young people as well as in facilitating transitions to citizenship and belonging (Cassity & Gow, 2005). With the dramatic increase of a migrant influx into our country, there is an urgent need to educate them fairly and appropriately. Although researchers have spotlighted the problems and inadequacies in providing educational support to these students, additional scholarship is needed that focuses on how to best serve them. Studying this problem can result in a positive contribution that offers solutions to the problem rather than merely examining the forlorn issue that continues to expand.

The principal focus of this inquiry was ascertaining best practices for educating the U.S. migrant student population. The Federal Office of Migrant Education was established to remediate the academic deficiencies that many migrant students face. The number of migrant students who lack English language proficiency or require remedial instruction is large. Their burden is multiplied as migrant parents have the lowest levels of education of any other occupational group. Considering that migrant students have the highest dropout rates in the nation, efforts to examine modes for their success are necessary in order to increase rates of graduation attainment.

As families continue to migrate into the United States, the teachers of migrant students must work in synergy with their students and their families as well as community partners to create systems of support and success. With migrant students becoming more of the norm in a growing number of classrooms nationwide, educators, school administrators and all educational stakeholders must recognize the realities of these students' experiences and unique needs. The major goal of this exploration was to identify what migrant students and their teachers see as hurdles, while isolating commonalities that will result in developing specific and strategic best practice approaches to intensify their graduation rates. Aware that there are evident gaps in the educational system that cause migrant students to not have the same opportunities, this probe led me to embrace the need to improve the skillset of educators in working with migrant students in classrooms across the country.

The equalitarianism mindset maintains that all members of the human race should be treated equally. In the realm of education, some students require additional, often individualized or differentiated support, to reach their maximum potentials. Migrant students are typically the farthest behind their peers and require exceptional instructional strategies in order to close the achievement gap. Resilience is required from students who feel both inadequate and incompatible as a result of their lack of English language acquisition and migratory lifestyle. While resilience is a key trait for anyone seeking success, leveling the playing field for those who need added help is true equity.

Researchers who have examined the course of migrant education have described migrant students as "invisible children" and one of the most helpless and disadvantaged groups of students due to the nature of their family's hardships when pursuing agricultural work in various counties and states. Their road to survival is endless as their mobility is dependent on circumstances beyond their control including weather, employment opportunities and harvesting patterns. As a result, migrant students are also overlooked because many live in temporary housing provided by their employers that is often secluded and miles away from the school. The hindrances and situations that complicate the identification and assessment process make it difficult to provide them with constant and ongoing support required by any student failing academically.

For decades, migrants have been one of the most academically vulnerable groups in the United States. The economic, health, and work-related problems they face result in lower levels of academic achievement and higher dropout rates. The working estimate of migrant student graduation rates in high school is roughly 45–50%, thus, there is a strong need for change in provided services, support, and standards for quality experiences.

The culture and lifestyle of migrant students differs from those of students born in this country and living at a permanent address. Migrant students using techniques that support their learning while including their way of living into the curriculum could enhance motivation needed to make them feel embraced by their teachers and peers. The majority of teachers in this country are White European-Americans. While that composition is slowly mutating, many lack training in teaching students who come from culturally diverse backgrounds and lack understanding of cultural norms that often can make a student feel uncomfortable, out of place, or isolated.

Bringing about a deeper understanding of how to best provide educational services to the migrant student population, is an obvious necessity. An approach that ensures an appropriate, adequate, and applicable educational experience is key to these students' success. Discovering parallels and corresponding attributes in what successful migrant students deem as invaluable to their achievement will be significant in the work that future educators will embark in. With limited information on mobile migrant students, school teachers might act more on the basis of negative stereotypes, fostering low expectations for academic performance and displaying a lack of investment in their progress. As educators learn to consider the individualized needs of this subgroup, mindsets and the success rate of these students can be transformed.

This prefatory chapter provides a justification for the need to explore and define specific and strategic best practices in the provision of migrant education. Defining migrant students and outlining their unique circumstances and difficulties is key to understanding the complexity of how to best improve amenities being delivered to them. The gaps in their education resulting from their frequent mobility make it a difficult trek toward their ultimate goal of graduation.

Dropping out of high school can lead to lost productivity, lower tax revenues, and a higher cost of public services with negative consequences for all students, not just those from migrant families. Providing quality-based opportunities for all students to succeed in the U.S. public education system exemplifies educational equity and social justice.

With the influx of people immigrating into the United States from all over the world, the country's demographics are changing. The majority of today's immigrants into the United States are from Central America, predominantly Mexico. Numbers from El Salvador, Honduras, Guatemala are also on the rise. Chinese and Indian immigrants round off the incoming migrant groups.

Resulting from the evolving demographics is an increase in diversity in our schools. These newly enrolled students come with their own gifts and talents, but their English language acquisition is nonexistent or minimal. Consequently, these new students require specific attention to meet their needs. A pedagogy of equity can only occur when teachers work to modify their teaching in order to facilitate the learning of students from different racial, cultural, and social-class groups.

With more than 650,000 children migrating across the United States year after year with their farmworker parents as they harvest fruits and vegetables, cultural and structural barriers are to be expected. Public schooling was not initially created with the backgrounds and experiences of the marginalized and poor in mind. As a result, migrant groups of students continue to receive below-par services, minimizing their success rates and lowering their attitudes about their capabilities. Past research on migrant students has shown these students struggle with self-esteem, depression, isolation, and rejection. This research was intended to enhance current systems and approaches with the sole goal of ensuring the students equity while capitalizing on what their experiences can lend to the classrooms of today.

Arguing for education that is uncompromising and deliberate as well as calculated and nurturing is the conceptual framework that drives providing migrant/ELL students with an educational program that is nothing less than productive. Within a neo-liberal policy framework, value is attributed to students who shape themselves to meet the neo-liberal ideal. In essence, only those students who contribute to their school's pool of talent are valued. This creates a tension for students in terms of how they position themselves in such a stress-filled, value-focused environment that is only concerned with state testing and data that illustrates high levels of performance. Rather than place the focus on high-stakes testing and the drilling of facts to close the achievement gap, schools must prioritize building a culture that supports the ideology that every student from every background has value. This paradigm shift will require a mindset that is both all-inclusive and creates a culture of student empowerment based on self-worth where everyone is seen as capable and respected.

Chapter Two

ROADBLOCKS ALONG THE MIGRANT ROUTE

M arginalized populations naturally find themselves struggling to survive, whether emotionally or financially. The experiences that they may or may not prevail in, with induced trauma can have lasting effects on the spirit within each of us. We are all built different, so some obstacles may seem larger than others and vice versa. To some, these "bumps in the road" can prove to be invigorating, to others they can be enough to kill the desire to want more. Unfortunately, most institutes of public education grapple with meeting the rare needs of the migrant student. The likelihood that advancements are made lay in the work of those on the front lines and their instructional leaders who rally alongside of them with the matching attitude of "all students matter even the temporary ones."

The prominent findings of the literature point at teacher attitude as an integral part of positively educating their migrant students. Several studies suggest a direct correlation between educators and their attitude or perception toward immigrants (Camata, Ybañez, De los Reyes, & Inocian, 2016). Effective teachers, however, can make the demanding situation seem less strenuous and viable learning possible. Lea (2012) explained that a teacher who best promotes his or her students is one with a cultural knowledge and understanding and open to making the adjustments required to provide their students an education adapted to their needs.

A study completed to analyze the No Child Left Behind Act (2001) revealed that many general education teachers also recognized the unsympathetic attitudes of fellow teachers who see their migrant/ELL students as "them" while making statements that describe these students as not belonging (Rouse, 2013). By confronting these attitudes and barriers, well-intentioned teachers can bring forth effective approaches for each of their deserving students. If schools are to be instrumental in the settlement process of incoming migrants, positive and welcoming attitudes to these students would appear to be essential (Taylor & Sidhu, 2012). Teachers of migrant students must remain sentient of the realities of living as a migrant student with their families in conditions that are less than adequate (Irizarry & Williams, 2013). Taylor and Sidhu (2012) conceded that despite the research that suggest what migrant teachers can and should do, there is limited research on what such teachers are actually doing to provide amicable and earnest support to migrant students.

Social capital through strong familial connections within the migrant community is a formidable theme throughout the research (Salinas, 2013). Relative to approaches used in working with migrant students, various studies cited teaching methods that complemented and interconnected with the cultural attributes of the migrant students that they worked to foster. For example, "homed-homelessness" is not a dichotomy for migrant students who travel in order to keep a home. For these students the concept of home differs from their peers and teachers who have never lived the migrant lifestyle (Nevarez-La Torre, 2011). To approach these students in a manner that is sensitive to their culture, changes in perceptions need to be made clear to all stakeholders who work with this unique population (Nevarez-La Torre, 2011).

LANGUAGE

The United Nations Educational, Scientific and Cultural Organization (UNESCO, 2018) conducted research across 26 countries showing that more than 50% of students who dropped out of school did not speak the language in which they were being educated. A 2012 report by the American Psychological Association noted that Latino students in the United States who spoke one language at home and another at school were at increased risk of graduating late or dropping out of high school (Vega, Laser & Plotts, 2015)

Language barriers coupled with limited community stays compound the challenges migrant students face as they try to fit into a public education system (Vocke, Westing, Applegate, & VanDonkelaar, 2016). Being proficient in the English language is essential in U.S. public schools (Crosnoe, 2006). When migrant students enter school with extremely limited English language acquisition their challenges are multiplied. Having to master academic content while simultaneously learning a new language is a grand expectation. Hakuta, Butler, and Witt (2000) maintained that it can take up to 2 years for most ELLs to learn social English, and that it can take 5 to 7 years or longer to master English in its academic format.

Not all language-minority students have the same trajectory for school success. Students who begin kindergarten with proficiency in English have academic trajectories similar to non-ELLs, whereas students who enter school at a later grade level with limited English proficiency do not fare as well, demonstrating weaker learning trajectories that are quite divergent from their non-English language learner peers by the end of elementary school (Vaughn et al., 2017).

Accompanying the achievement gap for these migrant ELLs is the critical issue that they are in need of high quality teachers in the classroom. The number of certified bilingual and English as a second language (ESL) teachers needs to increase and so does the instructional capacity of teachers serving ELLs in the mainstream classroom (Rodriguez, Abrego, & Rubin, 2014).

Migrant students may encounter vastly different teaching strategies in regards to learning English. School schools provide migrant students with English support while learning grade level content, other schools may only be learning English, and in still others they may be learning English with a simplified curriculum. The types of language support and availability of bilingual education that migrant students receive is crucial to how they learn English (Wright, 2010). Tellez and Varghese (2013) found that bilingual education teachers must possess a critical perspective as they are constantly working against political and social forces that seek to disempower, or at least not help to empower marginalized communities.

Social and Emotional Needs

While educational attainment is termed as achieving the highest level of schooling possible, educational well-being refers to having a nourishing environment that promotes educational attainment (Delgado & Herbst, 2017). The struggle of the migrant population is not only physically strenuous with the expectations of the hard labor of agricultural farm work but emotionally draining as well. For children, the emotional stress is multiplied as they spend their days in classrooms with strangers who look, speak and act differently. For weeks after a move, migrant families face the process of anonymization (Rodriguez-Valls & Torres, 2014). Nordstrom, McKibben, Baldauf, Tachieva, and Harding-Pittman (2012) described anonymization as a loss of identity particularly when issues of language and poverty exist. Because of the transitory and unstable nature of the migrant life, feelings of fear and temporary existence can have negative educational consequences (Free et al., 2014).

In conjunction with the feelings of non-belonging, youth from families who have immigrated into this county report high rates of stigmatization, distrust of authority figures, and feelings of hopelessness, anxiety, frustration, and dreading the future (Sulkowski, 2017). Having limited English proficiency not only hinders their academic progress but leads to social isolation (Grisham-Brown & McCormick, 2013). Fearing embarrassment as a result of their level of skill with the language, many students enrolled in migrant education programs avoid being vocal in class (Lorimer, 2016).

Early adolescence is a crucial phase in the educational trajectory of Latino/a youth as they make decisions between academic aspirations beyond high-school or a path of disengagement, poor performance and disruptive behavior (Delgado & Herbst, 2017). Given that 80% of immigrant children are at some point separated from their families, migrant youth are at risk for traumatization on the journey into the United States, acculturative stress and transgenerational damage (Phipps & Degges-White, 2014). These socio-emotional sufferings can be detrimental to educational attainment and other aspects of personal well-being (Suarez-Orozco & Suarez-Orozco, 2009).

Employing professionals who can provide appropriate emotional care to migrant students in a school setting is critical to meeting the unique needs of the whole migrant child. Teachers, guidance counselors, and school psychologists require the tools to manage a number of social and emotional needs. Fostering a sense of community that is inclusive of the emotional state of diverse groups that helps promote trust and respect is essential (Vega et al., 2015). The 2013–2014 National Agricultural Workers Survey reported the average level of completed education was eighth grade (National Center for Farmworker Health, 2017). If the focus is to graduate higher numbers of migrant students, meeting their basic needs is essential to their success. The disconnect that they experience between home and school culture must be addressed in order to elevate motivation while decreasing dropout rates.

Cultural Differences

Cultural barriers are evident differences between two or more cultures that lead to communication breakdowns and misunderstandings. The cultural barriers that exist between Mexican migrant students and their families and the school system often lead to educational challenges for migrant students. These cultural barriers may include students who do not make eye contact out of respect or parents who do not go to the school because they feel that would be disrespectful to the teacher. Several cultural barriers exist between migrant students, their families, and the school system. These barriers often bring about misperceptions that in turn lead to challenges for migrant students and their teachers. Alsubaie (2015) asserted that because the culture of teachers and students affect the education process, the relationship between culture and education is crucial. Because of the vitality of the link between culture and the educational setting, the education should reflect respect and be appropriate for students and their cultures in order to enhance achievement and build confidence (Alsubaie, 2015). The National Association for Multicultural Education (NAME; 2018) maintained that when students learn within a culturally diverse environment, a positive self-image develops as well as their way of thinking that develops their sense of self and value for their position in society.

Similar to their children in the classroom, parents of migrant students must learn to adapt to new cultural norms. These older family members bring their own opinions and insight about education, teachers, and the regard for each.

19

These ideologies are framed from their religious and cultural practices, their own schooling experiences, and the basis for leaving their country of origin (Adelman & Taylor, 2015). For many migrant parents, their previous experiences may have marred their trust in teachers and administrators, and institutional racism could have influenced their belief that higher education is a positive thing (Quiñones & Marquez-Kiyama, 2014). Consequently, when the migrant students learn to cope in the new environment at a faster rate than their migrant parent, they soon find themselves taking on adult tasks such as serving as a translator. This shift in roles adds to the stress of feeling adequate or capable (Adelman & Taylor, 2015).

Resources for Migrant Students

Schools working diligently to provide avenues for success for their migrant populations hire strategically to maximize support. Staffing schools with paraprofessionals who are able to communicate with their migrant students is vital to influencing knowledge attainment. Native-language support teachers' work with the expression "in the middle of a pedagogical triangle" through cooperation with the students and teachers and by acting as liaisons between the school and home (Virta, 2014). Despite the success of these support systems, the added staff can be costly and often difficult to find and schedule, particularly in schools where migrant populations were limited forcing staff to be shared across schools. Moreover, the ethno-specific staff feel vulnerable in their positions as they are commonly isolated from other teachers and treated as outsiders, much similar to the students that they are assigned to edify (Virta, 2014).

While placing qualified support staff is vital to the success of migrant students, their certified teachers are their greatest assets. As advocates for the learning of their students, the most beneficial educators of migrant children seek out any deficiencies. Although outright discrimination is not cited in the review of the literature, it can be perceived that many teachers do not understand their migrant students, and their lack of respect for their experiences triggers them to prune compassion (Free et al,, 2014). Migrant educators, especially those who have been migrant students in their earlier lives are able to share the same values and beliefs as well as incomparable experiential capital (Free & Križ, 2016). Migrant students, especially, should always believe there is trust and coherence in their education, as cultural conflicts can hinder their motivation and generate identity problems (Lea, 2012). Taylor and Sidhu (2012) asserted that the adoption of inclusive approaches for both teaching and learning is what makes for "good practice." By providing meaningful, genuine, and intensive language and learning support and then quickly mainstreaming then as they acquire basic literacy skills, students are made to feel like viable learners within their new campus (Taylor & Sidhu, 2012).

Principals and school leaders play a major role in the critical task of policy making and implementation for each of their migrant students. More vital are the classroom teachers who interact on a more personal and primary level with their students (Ficarra, 2017). Their training and development centered on issues of multiculturalism and the experiences of the migrant lifestyle are needed before attending to academic needs (Ficarra, 2017). Other works specify that in-classroom learning is not enough, but that teachers should participate in service-learning within the refugee community as part of their teacher preparation program (Lund & Lee, 2015). Ficarra (2017) maintained that while many advocate for collaboration when supporting migrant students, few seem to be writing about such collaborative work, perhaps due to the complexity of proper and effective collaboration that includes all stakeholders.

Instrumental in establishing some continuity in the instruction of many migrant students are countless summer migrant education programs (SMEDs) ready to take in students who have traveled to follow agricultural employment. Typical SMED programs provide students with interventions in specific content areas, opportunities for credit accrual and individualized instruction to practice and enhance reading skills (Vocke et al., 2016). Even with the best intentions, however, the program directors cited inconsistent program evaluations, availability of services, and differences in state educational requirements as barriers to maximizing their effectiveness. In general, migrant programming is varied in its focus and its success, mostly due to a lack of consistent and organized research (Vocke et al., 2016)

With nearly one third of the country's migrant students living in California, the state established the Migrant Student Information Network (MSIN) for the purpose of providing appropriate supports to this penurious population (Miller, 2017). Through this network, the systems in place allow educational stakeholders expedited access to accurate and updated information relative to the student's academic history, saving weeks of time that can be taken up tracking and locating such data (Miller, 2017). Because not every migrant student is fortunate enough to be tracked via the MSIN, migrant educators often are forced to undertake added administrative duties to help guide their migrant students through the school system (Free & Križ, 2016). Tasks include identifying them as eligible for MEP services, ensuring that they receive language testing, and appropriate credit transfers (Free & Križ, 2016). As noble as the efforts are, there is a dire need for a universal system that tracks each migrant student in a reliable and accessible format.

As these migrant students come to school with none or limited English skills, approaches to accelerate and extend their progress have been employed with restricted success. Troia (2014) highlighted the Fast ForWord Language program, a computer-based intervention program designed to swiftly develop auditory-perceptual and spoken language communicative competence. While both the preliminary and secondary experimental clinical studies were encouraging, the results did not merit efficacy for the program (Troia, 2014). Additionally, Troia (2014) cited the research as inconclusive as the measurement protocols were inconsistent in measuring literacy achievement. Thus, the FFW data should be reviewed and examined with caution. The research itself, however, played a key role in comparing direct instruction to that of a computer program relative to supporting ELLs.

LIMITATIONS TO SUPPORTING MIGRANT STUDENTS

Families who are vulnerable to U.S. Immigration policies are reluctant to interact with any group that could reveal their immigration status. These families require the education system to lead efforts that work to assist and stabilize this susceptible yet promising group of students. Because the research indicates that having an unauthorized immigration status is an affront to students' academic success, tactics to develop these students and to build trusting relationships with them and their families must be differentiated (Sulkowski, 2017). Schools must also work to connect their migrant families with agencies specific to their needs. Sulkowski (2017) contended while being mindful of the worries of their migrant assignments, educational leaders should focus on linking them to social service agencies, human rights workers, immigration attorneys, or any organization working directly to aid immigrants, regardless of their status.

The literature discusses limitations and inconsistencies in past studies about how to best meet the needs of migrant students. Because of the mobility of these students, much of the data are inconclusive or involve small sample sizes, which restrains the scope of each study. Often many of these students entered the country or migrated at different times or frequencies and have undergone an array of experiences. Thus, additional studies would be required to confirm the stability of any reported findings (Makarova & Herzog, 2013). Likewise, dependent on their immigration status or comfort level with the researchers, information disclosed within interviews or surveys may not be accurate (Carter,

Reschly, Lovelace, Appleton, & Thompson, 2012). Moreover, as programs are put into action, financial support is essential for their maintenance and sustainability in order to actively employ models and approaches to empower migrant students and their families (Free & Križ, 2015).

Much attention has been given to cultural, linguistic and mental health hindrances; however, the disproportionate interest in identifying the most effective approaches to minimizing these barriers is alarming. Identifying the struggles of migrant students is imperative to distinguishing and isolating programs, modalities and tactics to curtail the obstacles and maximize the potential of every migrant student. Migrate through the subsequent chapters for honest insight into the loves of former farmworker students and what they indicate as ingredients necessary to take them to higher levels of academic success.

Chapter Three

Let's Take Attendance: From Migrant to Magnificent

M eet the former migrant students who have now earned college degrees. Their first-hand accounts on the life of the migrant student are both eye-opening and central to supporting their younger counterparts seeking the same academic accomplishments.

Margarita

A graduate of the University of Notre Dame, with a master's degree in education, Margarita and her family migrated to pick both watermelon and corn in the state of Georgia during the summer months. She cited her parents as instrumental in her success as they saw an importance in education. They illustrated this by only having her and her siblings migrate during non-school months, whenever possible. Teachers who taught her to set small attainable goals and that pushed her to respond and participate in class discussions were noted as positively influential. For Margarita, success in school was catapulted by teachers who worked to not make her feel less than anyone else. Her favorite teachers acknowledged her and saw her migrant lifestyle as something that made her unique, rather than use it to take away from who she was. As a migrant student, however, not all of her experiences were positive.

> *"I remember feeling really out of place, like I was behind. I was always less likely to respond during lessons, because I felt like I hadn't built that rapport and was scared of my teachers."*

Margarita taught middle school in Texas for several years and now serves as a human resources manager for a statewide nonprofit that provides childcare and education to several thousand migrant children each year. Reflecting on her education, she affirmed that today's teachers need to create discussions on diversity so that everyone is represented. In her estimation, teachers who don't invest in each one of their students are not investing in themselves as effective educators. For Margarita, teaching migrant students the value of having grit and to not be deterred by the constant changes in schools can be influential in helping them beat the odds.

> *"You have to visualize your path and that is part of the challenge especially when your parents don't understand what it takes or means to be successful educationally. You are overwhelmed*

and often don't know where to start. Having a visual and setting goals of what need to be done in order to get from here to there is essential."

Tomàs

Now an operations manager at Amazon, Tomàs most respected the educators who pushed him while refusing to accept excuses. His most memorable teacher catered to the varying learning styles and Tomàs respected the manner in which he would interact with all students. Never feeling left out, this particular educator was consistently uplifting, boosting his esteem. Learning English was a barrier for him, but he accomplished it as a result of inducements and motivational experiences. Tomàs appreciated recognitions and awards, academic competitions, reading incentive programs and opportunities that encouraged him to contend for accolades.

"Getting a certificate for reaching a goal did so much for me. Every time I earned one it reminded me that I was capable. I still have every single one of them."

Never wanting to let anyone down, especially those who emboldened him, he acknowledged that when teachers go above and beyond, it creates a sense of reciprocation.

Tomàs opined that teachers of migrant students must be willing to understand their perspective and nurture them towards seeing themselves as capable. Always appreciating extrinsic rewards, he also regarded intrinsic support as critical. Grateful for graduating both high school and college, both were achievements that he never saw as happening early in his education. The teachers who built him up with confidence made all of the difference. Obtaining his bachelor's degree from Colgate University, Tomàs is working toward his MBA as the striving continues when the thriving is in place.

Carmen

Carmen's father passed away when she was just three years old. The migrant life was all her mother knew, and it was the life that they continued to live in order to keep food on the table. Traveling from Florida to Georgia to Michigan and then back to Florida, Carmen remembered picking varying crops alongside her mother. Because she often missed school, Carmen always felt she had to work twice as hard.

> *"Playing catch-up in school seemed to be how I always lived my life growing up. It was draining, it was discouraging, and it never seemed fair."*

She had decided to quit school in the ninth grade until Ms. Nelson, a speech teacher, helped her discover her talents and see herself as capable. Ms. Nelson pushed her to apply to college. She was accepted to Florida Gulf Coast University where she earned her bachelor's degree in social work. Carmen is now a graduate student at the University of South Florida working toward her master's degree via an advanced standing program, which will allow her to graduate in twelve months.

Carmen attributed her accomplishments to her mother, coupled with the services of the migrant resource center at her high school. Her mother constantly reminded her that "education is the way out." Although her mother was seldom able to attend parent conferences, Carmen knew that her mother valued the benefits of teaching and learning. The support that her mother could not provide was subsidized by a resource center housed at her high school campus. Specifically designed for migrant students, the center provided her with school supplies and access to technology and tutoring.

"Having all of the necessary resources is important. When you have what you need to get the job done, then you are on the same playing field with everyone else. You no longer feel like an outcast."

Carmen credited site-based programs like the one at her alma mater for making sure that she was equipped with what she needed, while simultaneously alleviating the stresses of her already harrowing lifestyle.

Mateo

Serving today as the vice president of a prominent local bank branch, Mateo cited his work ethic as his greatest attribute. Working in the fields and migrating year after year while in elementary school opened his eyes to what defines hard work. He was retained in first grade because his family's summer migration pattern did not allow him to attend summer school. In high school he recalled his guidance counselor providing much needed emotional support after being told by a teacher that he was not cut out for college. The guidance counselor's advocacy provoked him to apply and eventually earn a scholarship. He explained,

> *"Those migrant students who dropout have the work ethic and grit to achieve, but they don't have anyone there to tell them what they need and the resources available to get there."*

Immediately after high school graduation, Mateo was diagnosed with cancer. For most, this would signal the end to a positive future, but after coming this far, quitting was no longer an option. As planned, he moved four hours away to live the next four years in his college dorm. He began his first semester of college while undergoing chemotherapy, and his desire to prove himself pushed him through to graduation. Today, Mateo holds a bachelor's degree in business administration from the University of Florida with specific licensures from the Florida School of Banking. The favorite part of his job involves community involvement. Giving back to others who are now where he once was is what drives him to continue to dream big.

> *"As adults who have been through serious struggles, we have to make the time to reach out and tell the next generation that they too can go far. The right words can go far."*

Amancia

The recollection of travelling to Georgia each year to pick watermelons was still vibrant in Amancia's memory. The family tried leaving school a month or two early each year in order to bring back watermelons to sell at the farmer's market so they would not have to move over and over each year. Her family would take turns travelling to bring back loads of watermelons, simultaneously keeping her from attending school. During this time period she was either picking watermelons or selling them. Amancia credited her self-confidence from her days of selling.

> *"Talking to people I had never met and persuading them to buy from us really got me out of my shell. This is how I learned to speak out and developed my outgoing personality."*

This poise and self-assurance drove her to apply to college. After being accepted to Michigan State University as part of their College Assistance Migrant Program (CAMP), Amancia continued her employment as a migrant farmworker when she could not find a summer job. Having earned a bachelor's degree in human development and family studies, she now wanted to work with students and families to educate and provide them with the resources necessary to break the cycle of poverty. She is currently employed as a postsecondary advocate where she supervises and tracks the academic success of 75 minority students. Her role allowed her to be a motivator and advocate for students who may not know where to find the help that they need.

In middle school and high school, Amancia was extremely interested in history. She maintains that teachers of migrant students should work purposefully to keep classrooms diverse, using the students' backgrounds as teaching points. Adding that many history textbooks are one-sided and that various cultures are not portrayed across the content areas, she believed that today's educators must provide them with such experiences even if it requires digging. She acknowledged parental support as instrumental to her accomplishments. She clarified that while parents are key, migrant students often must push themselves due to the sacrifices that are often made to make ends meet.

"Teachers often think less of our parents because they don't show up to parent night or report card pickup night. It isn't that education is not a priority. In fact it is the opposite. If they don't work, bills don't get paid and their children suffer. Teachers need to realize that not everyone works a 9 to 5 schedule and can take off in the middle of the day to meet with a teacher."

Rigoberto

Having earned a bachelor's degree in criminology and sociology from Ohio State University, Rigoberto now serves as a case manager in the Ohio attorney general's office in the consumer protection department. He chose this profession to help those who do not have the resources or capabilities to help themselves. He connected his work of today as a give-back for all of those who did the same for him and his family. Enduring the necessity to travel from Georgia to South Carolina and then to Tennessee and Virginia to harvest tomatoes and peppers, he needed huge support to fill the gaps when he reenrolled in school. The teachers who saw him as more than a temporary student made an impact on him.

"Strangely enough, I was always grateful to be a migrant student. Travelling was how I learned about tolerance and tenacity. I understood that it was part of what my family did and I could either hate it or embrace it."

While he conceded that his parents always pushed him to persevere, he acknowledged the certain type of teacher that stirred his thirst to succeed. Animated teachers who made him feel no less than his classmates and who were consistently positive were his favorite.

Rigoberto considered it an honor to have experienced the life of a migrant student. The strong friendships that he made were just as numerous as the schools he attended, especially those made at the high school level. He credits school fieldtrips and engaging classroom experiences for exciting him instead of distressing him when it was time to change schools. Knowing that a new environment meant new opportunities to learn and see things helped to keep him enthused. A lover of books, Rigoberto always had one in hand and appreciated those teachers who understood his passion and made sure that he had plenty of books to read as he traveled to his next venture. The teachers who respected him as a genuine person and not just a transient student helped to shape not only his personality but his candid zest for life.

Estella

Following the harvest was an opportunity for Estella to meet new people, explore new cultures, and see the "real world." Estella explained that tackling adversity with an optimistic attitude was key to her earning her Bachelor of Science degree in nursing from Nova Southeastern University. She remembered always starting school out of state and then coming back to her home as soon as the local crops were ready for harvesting. Spanish was her primary language and she recalled how it impeded her learning.

"It wasn't enough that I missed school for weeks at a time. Not being able to speak English made everything so much harder."

Paired with the learning gaps from the constant migration, her struggle was multiplied. Through it all, she set goals for herself and then raised the bar each time she met them. The goal of earning no grade lower that a C soon transformed to earning straight A's.

Estella cites her success in school as being dependent on each one of her teachers. If a teacher treated her well and made purposeful attempts at helping guide her to catch up and master skills, she returned the favor by giving her all.

"Failing or succeeding for me was often dependent on the teacher. For some reason, the teachers who were kind and patient were the ones who inspired me to push myself harder. The teachers that I remember most are the ones who sat me down and made sure I was on track to move forward. They would even give up their own lunch time to help me."

Explaining that a love for something pushes one to transmit it to others, Estella believes that students have to be willing to work as well. Feeling accomplished, she was always compelled to repay her parents for their sacrifices. This was always her motivation. In respect to teachers of migrant students, she expects that they must take the time to understand the situation of their students, provide them with appropriate resources and treat them as able and knowledgeable.

Maricela

A teacher today, it was Maricela's educational experiences as a migrant student that stirred her to ensure that today's migrant students receive the quality experiences that they whole-heartedly deserve. She remembered that learning English was one of her first goals. Begging her older brother to teach her at every available opportunity, she became fluent rapidly, allowing her to excel in school despite changing schools from year to year. Migrating from Florida to South Carolina, whenever and wherever work was available, she never felt treated different. On the contrary, she always felt that the non-Migrant students always wanted to hear and learn about her lifestyle. While she admitted that her experience was not the norm, she is well aware that for most migrant students, the experience is highly dependent on the teacher and student resilience.

> *"I was lucky in that my mom knew the importance of education and she did what she could to make sure that I didn't fail. She would often call on the neighbors who were a bit more proficient to come over and tutor me."*

As a teacher with a master's degree in curriculum and instruction from the University of Florida, Maricela cognized the need to hold all students to the same high standard. She explained that all students are qualified to learn and progress; however, some students who have gaps in learning may need extra time or support.

> *"A good teacher meets the students where they are, regardless of where they come from."*

While teaching gives Maricela much satisfaction, she feels the need to leave the walls of her classroom and go out into the community to mentor and get involved. She believed this should be the practice of all teachers in the hope of building strong rapports with both students and families. In her estimation, compassion and empathy can do much to propel migrant student engagement and feelings of self-worth.

Javier

Enrolling in three different schools each school year was typical for Javier and his family. Following the seasons of the harvest was their only means of income considering both of his parents were high school dropouts. Growing up, he would have never thought he would hold a master's degree in architecture. Referencing his unpredictable and always changing locale, Javier described his frustrations with not being able to commit to much of anything.

> *"Playing sports or joining a club was never an option because I never knew how long I was going to stay in one place. It was the same for making friends or getting comfortable in a classroom."*

Luckily for Javier, he found his passion in art and found it to be familiar from school to school yet varied enough to excite him as he continuously migrated. His skills in math, coupled with his adoration for all things art, is what steered him to seek a future as an architect.

"Working in the fields taught me that I didn't want to get a job just to earn money. It pushed me to aspire to do something that I loved."

Javier membered the first time his parents genuinely considered his art skills as impressive and backed his decision to pursue a college career. Despite their financial struggles, his parents always made sure that he had what he needed so that he would never consider calling it quits. He whole-heartedly noted that teachers of migrant students should always take this same stance, explaining,

"With all of the changes with moving, it is hard to prioritize school. Teachers need to understand that there are barriers and provide available resources so that the transitions are as smooth as possible."

Luciano

As a child Luciano never thought he would attend college. His family consistently traveled to the Florida panhandle to pick tomatoes and then back to South Florida to harvest saw palmetto berries. He was active in sports, but they never took priority over his responsibility of pitching in to help pay the family's bills. His ultimate goal was graduating high school, until he began to use the resources of his high school's migrant center, which gave him resources like paper and use of the computer lab; more importantly, the staff understood his predicament but believed in his capabilities. Although he was fluent in English, his confidence was minimal, sensing that farm work and agriculture would be his career.

"The teachers in the migrant center knew how to make me see myself as more than a farmworker. They even met with my parents so that they could understand the opportunities available to me."

The Migrant Center connected Luciano with Michigan State University and their college assistance migrant program (CAMP). Nervous about the transition, the university's CAMP program provided a liaison as well as a mentor to ensure that Luis never felt alone or overwhelmed.

"Not only did the program help pay for my books and other expenses, but they also helped me to get acclimated and comfortable with the college lifestyle."

Today Luis holds a bachelor's degree in interdisciplinary studies and hopes to move forward towards a focus on psychology. His future aspiration is to provide critical therapy to individuals who need it most.

"One-on-one help is what got me to where I am today. The fact that caring people took the time

to support and encourage me made all of the difference in the world."

Federico

Becoming a certified public accountant was always Federico's dream job. Doing it in our nation's capital, for an elite finance company, while earning more in a month than his parents earned in a year was nothing that he could have imagined.

"I am an example of hard work paying off," is how he described his success story.

Federico's parents came to the United States from Mexico, and Spanish was his first language. The oldest of six children, he was the first to toil in the fields, picking tomatoes alongside his parents. He remembers being paid by the bucket and calculating his family's earnings in his head as they worked.

"We were paid 25 cents for each bucket of tomatoes that we picked. I was constantly tallying how much we had made and how much more we needed to pick to meet our daily goal."

An aficionado of mathematics, numbers always excited him. Because he was good at them, he knew that he could use his skills to excel in school and seek a career relative to his adoration. As he learned English, he came to understand that math was universal. Shifting from school to school, he never worried about not doing well in math class.

"Being good at math gave me a sense of confidence. Even though I wasn't the best reader, I was always the best in math. The others students would ask me for help in math and I made lots of friends this way. I never felt like I didn't fit in or as if I wasn't as valued."

Federico believes that because of his strong number sense, teachers never saw him as incompetent. In retrospect, he sees his migrant experiences as positive and is thankful that attending various schools allowed him to see himself as adept in a broader setting.

"When I saw that I was good at math everywhere I went, I learned a lot about my capacity."

He shares that when teachers of migrant students treat them as able and teachable, they will rise to the challenge. While attending Florida State University, Federico took on tutoring dozens of fellow students in all areas of math and recalled how these efforts helped to subsidize his scarce income.

Rosalinda

Rosalinda described herself as "intuitive and curious." With a degree in criminology, both of these descriptors were perfect for her choice of career. Now working as a juvenile probation officer, she acknowledged her attributes for helping her succeed as a young student. In her work with the criminal justice system, she tells others about her struggles and help them to understand that hard work and perseverance is the only formula for success. Rosalinda came to the United States from Mexico when she was 11 years old. Her first school quickly immersed her in the English language and she recalled having to pick it up quickly in order to survive.

> *"There was no one to translate for me and my teacher talked to me a lot with her hands. I always wanted to learn, so I wasn't shy and used the limited English that I did know to get by."*

Within a couple of years Rosalinda learned the language and showed promise in all academic areas. Her best memories involved learning new phrases and teaching her non-Hispanic peers Spanish. The teachers who did not accept excuses and challenged her to make gains were instrumental in her success.

> *"It was just me and my mom and while she worked the fields I had to pull my weight in the classroom. No matter how hard school seemed, I always knew that her long days in the hot sun were always harder."*

Because she was an avid learner by nature, Rosalinda noted the transitions from school to school were not difficult. Her curiosity allowed her to explore and learn from her new surroundings. Her optimistic attitude reminded her of how lucky she was to be part of a country that she respected and appreciated. Her life in Mexico was a world of difference. Her mother fled the country and her abusive father and consistently promised her that everything was going to be okay. Only in high school did she learn her academic performance was on par to get her into college. She always did well in school, but always thought that she would never be able to catch up with her peers. Still speaking with an obvious accent and never learning how to write in cursive, she just assumed that graduating high school would be her greatest achievement. Unique services provided to migrant students in her high school swiftly changed her mindset. Tutoring for college admission tests prepared her well. Additionally, the migrant program provided her with a tour of several colleges, which worked to intensify her desire to further her education.

~~~~~~~~~

The students acknowledged their own prior learning gaps and told of their frustration when the learning was either repeated or unconnected to prior schooling. As young students they did not understand that the gaps were beyond their control, and as a result they developed stigmas that decreased their motivation. Irizarry and Williams (2013) noted that support for migrant students with learning gaps requires more that foundational skills and grade-level content expectations. Explaining to students the cause of their academic lags, rather than allowing them to believe that they are incapable, could have saved them from unnecessary anxiety. Romanowski (2003) supported this idea, contending that obstacles to the success of migrant students stem from teachers' lack of understanding of their own beliefs about migrant students, which are influenced by prejudices that guide their behavior and actions.

Banks (1993) argued teachers must resist seeing multicultural education as merely content integration; rather, it should be viewed as a restructuring that allows all students to acquire knowledge, attitudes, and skills required to function with success in a diverse world. These particular migrant students revealed positive experiences in which the teachers used their unique travelling experiences and backgrounds to help make connections, build trust, and bring them in as bona fide contributors to their classroom. This notion supports Kugler (2018), who suggested schools must shift their focus from using high-stakes testing and fact drilling to narrow the achievement gap and build a culture that supports the ideology that every student from every background has value. Each one of the student participants cited respectful teachers who treated them as learners with potential as a major contributor to their success.

The resources available to the student participants proved to be not only powerful but greatly appreciated. While past research has focused on summer migrant education programs rather than the on campus migrant center experienced by the participating students, their purpose for helping migrant students "catch up" are identical. The students consider themselves lucky to have attended a high school campus that provided the migrant center as a resource.

Unfortunately, such programs are limited in both location and funding. Torrez (2014) asserted that without proper funding, support, or resources, attempts to take migrant students to advanced levels of education will fail to support them in realizing their potential.

While each success story varied, each convoluted trail resulted in triumph, proving that success is not selective. It is not the deck of cards that is dealt to one that matters, but rather the way the hand is played, and even replayed when the game ends in a loss. Recognizing that losing is part of the game, is essential. It is only when you quit trying, that you truly lose. For these determined gladiators, the spirit to prevail was at the forefront of their victories. Coupled with teachers who shared the same spirit, the concoction for amazing results was laid out, as if by fate. Let's meet the educators who were significant in igniting fires, building genuine rapports with these students and vested in being actively engaged in the teaching and learning process.

Chapter Four

The Teachers that Mattered: Impactful and Integral

The following educators were cited by their former students as *extraordinary in their field. Mentioned by name, they each left everlasting effects in the lives of migrant students.*

Mrs. Sanchez

The crux of Mrs. Sanchez's mindset regarding migrant students is that academic achievement is not beyond reach with proper parental support, school resources, strong and structured classrooms, and their innate drive. According to Sanchez,

> *"Being outperformed by their non-migrant peers is no longer the norm. Every student has had some type of struggle, but what is unique about*

migrant students is that they have been faced with struggles and learned early on about work ethic and grit."

A former migrant student herself, Mrs. Sanchez realized how her experiences in farm-work molded her into the person that she is today. She is a prime example of the capabilities of migrant students and understands that building strong rapports and going beyond the walls of the classroom are the recipe for motivation. Her idea that bringing learning to life is derived from the various learning she acquired travelling the agricultural route and experiencing new communities.

Mrs. Rickard

Understanding the reasons for learning gaps in migrant students is the first step for Mrs. Rickard whenever providing services to her migrant students. Mistakenly believing that migrant work ended after the Great Depression, she was fascinated and intrigued when she taught her first group of migrant students. As she worked to identify learning gaps, she was frustrated with the tracking of data.

"I wish that the education system was better at tracking student progress across district and state lines. Teachers who receive new migrant students have no idea what curriculum, standards or assessments were used with them."

Additionally, Mrs. Rickard saw the current political atmosphere as an additional challenge for migrant students. She noted the fear of deportation and family separation increases stress and anxiety of frequently moving and changing schools.

Mr. Gonzalez

A lead resource teacher in a high school migrant center, Mr. Gonzalez worked daily with migrant students in an effort to close the gap and best prepare them for graduation. The philosophy in the center is founded on individualization. Gonzalez believed the most successful students are the ones that take full advantage on the resources available to them. While some of the migrant students that he had worked with must be strongly encouraged to use its services, those who triumph are the ones who take full advantage of all of their services, enthusiastically and willingly.

"Self-motivation is key and is what can make or break a student's exit from high school."

Mrs. Garza

As a high school counselor, Mrs. Garza recognized the need to get to know her migrant population. Establishing an open line of communication, not only with the students but with their parents, so that everyone understands the power of education, the available resources and the need to set goals is her methodology for creating success stories. As she saw it,

> *"The key is to develop an atmosphere, from school to home, where the migrant students feel comfortable and understood."*

Garza believed that with the right motivation, guidance, and opportunities, migrant students have infinite professional potential. She asserted that migrant parents are no different than non-migrant parents in that they want what is best for their children. "They know how hard migrant work can be and they certainly don't want that for their kids."

Mr. Wells

Working with migrant students for more than 25 years, Mr. Wells had witnessed the dependent learning style that most of them possess. Mr. Wells found that many rewards come from educating this unique group; however, he acknowledged that it can be very taxing emotionally.

> *"They will invest in you as long as you are personally invested. I found that in addition to teaching them it is important to take an interest in their lives."*

Additionally, Wells believed if a teacher understands a student's home life the teacher can better relate to the student's needs. Wells suggested that rigid classroom plans and too much structure can put them in unfamiliar situations, which in turn make the teaching and learning more difficult.

Mr. Bodisson

Now a high-school principal, Mr. Bodisson used his former classroom experience when working with teachers to hone their skills. Modeling as much as possible is his most critical piece of advice that he passes on to the teachers that he evaluates, noting:

> *"Questioning, probing, and explaining your thinking is necessary when teaching migrant students. Once you see a student struggling, it is always important to pull that student aside, one on one, to incorporate whatever strategy works best for them."*

As an administrator, Bodisson utilizes the same strategy to best understand students dealing with behavioral issues, understanding that each student is unique and requires individualized attention.

Collectively, these teachers who had each been successful in working with migrant students echoed the need to understand the struggle of the migrant family. The teachers revealed the need to approach their migrant students with caution because of the unique strains that moving and adapting to new situations can put on a child. Free (2016) argued that, as a result of their transient and unstable lifestyle, feelings of fear and temporary existence can negatively impact students' education. The teachers asserted that upon understanding what students endure in order to survive, an effective and caring teacher will work to remove the fears and bring about a sense of belonging. Relative to feelings of non-belonging, migrant students report high rates of stigmatization, distrust of authority figures, and feeling of anxiety, frustration, and dreading the future (Sulkowski, 2017). Maslow (as cited in McLeod, 2017) acknowledged that human motivation is based on an individual's needs being met. Ensuring that children's basic needs are met is vital in all classrooms. Respectively, each of the educators who took part, shared educational philosophies grounded in Maslow's theory and saw it as imperative, especially in children of poverty and where English is a second language.

Teachers of migrant students must also determine where to begin with instruction with respect to their children's learning gaps. Irizarry and Williams (2013) cited research suggesting that migrant children, because of their academic lags, require more than typical delivery of curriculum. The teachers within this chapter suggested they had to identify learning gaps and implement strategic methods to guide students to close those gaps while bridging them with new or common skills.

As the diversity of the student migrant population continues to grow, systems to support them educationally must be prepared to support the best practices for optimal results (Grisham-Brown & McCormick, 2013). Being successful with their migrant students, the highlighted teachers echoed the required extra efforts beyond the school day, citing that training and support is essential for teachers struggling to make gains with this unique population.

Consequently, the teacher participants expressed a great deal of gratitude for the migrant resources and support that they had been allotted. Confirming that the task of best educating a migrant student requires a team of compassionate and skilled professionals, the teachers understood that schools where some of their students came from may not have had the added resources. Virta (2014) explained that despite the success of these support systems, the added staff can be costly and difficult to find and schedule, especially in schools where migrant populations are limited.

Chapter Five

Theme One: The Need to Understand the Migrant Student Lifestyle

Lack of empathy for our instability

Student participants found that those teachers who took the time to learn about and understand their journeys as migrant students were easier to trust and learn from. In contrast, student participants who experienced negative treatment from teachers who were unable to empathize with their situation recalled those experiences as detrimental. Amancia shared that she was observant and could tell when a teacher was sincere.

"I was fortunate to have had some very thoughtful teachers and it was easy to tell when

a teacher was not happy about getting a new student in the middle of a semester. You could tell it was a burden for them."

Had they taken the opportunity to consider the burdens endured by the migrant student, perhaps their approach would have been different. For Rigoberto, an empathetic teacher was a true teacher.

"I just wanted to learn and when I came into a new class and felt welcomed by the teacher I was ready to learn."

Feelings of not belonging

It is understandable that when people have no permanent home, it can be difficult to find their place. The migrant student participants echoed this sentiment repeatedly, explaining that feeling "out of place" was traumatic each time they entered a new school, often two or three times every school year. Carmen explained that these feelings were heightened when she was pulled out for remediation.

"I already had anxiety because I felt like an outsider, and then I was pulled out for tutoring and I never really got to make friends or even connect with my teacher."

Margarita experienced this level of alienation to a minimum in grade school and high school; however, she recalled experiencing it at a much higher-degree in college, where most of her classmates were non-Hispanic.

"For me, it wasn't until I entered college that I learned about feeling isolated and indifferent."

These experiences influenced the way that she interacted with the migrant students that she taught when she went into the teaching profession. A sense of belonging, no doubt, improves motivation and happiness and for migrant students it can be the difference in success or failure.

EMPATHY AND COMPASSION FOR ALL STUDENTS

Relative to making efforts to understand the migrant lifestyle, the teacher participants echoed their role in developing connections with ALL students. Mrs. Garza concurred that while all students require kindness and understanding, migrant students require a level of empathy and compassion that is sincere and well-intended.

"Because they are already facing so many struggles and hardships at home, school should be a place where they feel understood, where they are embraced and where they are respected."

Mr. Wells has a parallel conviction:

"Migrant students tend to be very dependent learners. They will invest only as long as you as a teacher are personally invested. It is emotionally taxing to teach migrant students and do a good job."

Making connections is fundamental

Several of the teacher participants spoke Spanish, which they cited as useful in helping them make connections with their migrant students. They recognized that this alone helps with establishing connections and makes the teaching process easier when translation is needed. Non-Spanish speaking teacher Mr. Bodisson contended that building strong, positive relationships, believing in students, and showing them that you do care helped him to be a successful teacher. Growing up as a migrant student herself, Mrs. Sanchez always shared with her migrant students her experiences allowing them to see that there is hope.

"Not only did I share my story, but I never shied away from giving them hugs and telling them I loved them."

Teachers unanimously discussed how making connections on a personal level increased the level of engagement of their migrant students, helping them to dispel fears and trust issues.

Interviewed participants agreed that teachers need to make a genuine effort to grasp a better understanding of what it means to be a migrant and how their lifestyle can effect learning. Javier recalled coming in to class tired from working the packing house the night before and the teachers who allowed him to take a nap during his lunch period. Another would bring him chocolate to improve his energy. For Estella, when a favorite teacher took the time to visit her home when she was having trouble getting to school, she began to believe that she mattered.

"When she took the time to understand and provide me and my family with some help, I knew that my education was just as important as everyone else's."

Mr. Wells, now retired and proud of his work with migrant students, added that getting to know the students is obligatory.

"Migrant kids will include you in their lives where other students see you as intruding."

Formerly a migrant student and now an educator herself, Maricela saw empathy as a nonnegotiable when working with migrant students:

"Sharing another person's emotions from a different perspective is powerful in building connections. When a teacher makes the time and takes the time to see where these students are

coming from and all that they have to struggle with, a heightened willingness to bring about real change is sparked."

Mrs. Sanchez echoed the need for compassion and understanding.

"As simple as it sounds, patience and empathy need to be used because most migrant students come with much baggage and struggles. We have to let them know that this is ok and we need to teach them to use this baggage and struggle as part of their journey that they will hopefully continue to use as fuel. Some educators still look down at baggage and struggle as downfalls, but we need to see them as stepping stones and we need to be more open-minded."

Mr. Gonzalez asserted that establishing a comfort level with both the students and their parents is strategic and vital.

"Once our migrant students feel comfortable enough to ask questions and seek assistance, the teaching process becomes easier."

Chapter Six

Theme Two: Individualized and Supplemental Instruction Works to Close Learning Gaps

Patience and genuine concern for success is critical

Migrant students often arrive at new schools behind academically. The issue is typically the misalignment of standards and expectations from state to state. Teachers interviewed found that migrant students are extremely capable and that patience when guiding them to fill their gaps is critical. Mrs. Rickard admitted that teachers need additional training about migrant students and their unique situations. She herself always mistakenly believed that migrant work ended decades prior. It wasn't until she began to work with migrant students that she came to learn about their unique situations.

> *"Once I learned the cause of their gaps, I became concerned about the lack of equity in their education and understood that I had to approach them with patience as I tackled knowledge gaps."*

As a result of their migratory lifestyle, migrant students have witnessed an array of dispositions and have learned to detect teachers who are genuinely on their side.

WORK ETHIC IS NOT THE PROBLEM

The student participants interviewed indicated that doing the work was never an obstruction for getting them on par with their non-migrant peers. The migrant lifestyle taught them grit and perseverance. The challenges that they faced outside of the classroom were minimal compared to completing assignments, taking on a new language, or learning new concepts. Mateo reported that migrant students know the need for hard work and are not less capable than other students their age.

> *"We have the work ethic and are disciplined, we just need the tools and direction to get us to the next level."*

Federico understood that because of his strong math skills, he was never labeled as incompetent, but saw his younger siblings suffer when some teachers tried to water down their instruction and treated them as inept:

> *"Not believing that a migrant student can perform as well or better than a non-migrant student is assuming that they are not smart enough. Our struggles have forced us to work hard and we will do that when the circumstances allow us to."*

Rosalinda, who considered herself lucky to have had competent teachers who cared and knew how to best approach her, understood that the learning gaps were inevitable.

> *"From school to school, I would learn something that I had either already learned or that I didn't understand. When I didn't understand, it was usually because I had missed something that was previously taught. My teachers were always good about picking up on this and made the time to catch me up."*

Luciano experienced similar mismatches in his migrant travels, but considered himself fortunate to have been a quick learner.

> *"I was always a good reader and never shy, so if I didn't get it I asked a teacher or a classmate. It*

was always extra work for me, but I was lucky to have had teachers that allowed me extra time or gave me extra support. They didn't just classify me as migrant and forgot about me. They found my strengths and worked on the areas where I was lacking."

MAKE EFFORTS TO ASSESS ACADEMIC LEVELS/COMPETENCIES

When migrant students enter a classroom several assumptions are made and most are left to catch on quickly and fend for themselves. Many schools do not or cannot offer specialized support to migrant students due to limited resources. While this is understood by the teachers interviewed, they collectively agreed that as their teacher you must meet migrant students where they are at and consider where the absences of knowledge are and create a plan of attack. Mrs. Rickard had worked with migrant students identified as gifted, so for her, assuming that they are unable solely based on their migrant status is unreasonable.

> *"I have had gifted migrant students who were the top performers in my class. Migrant students have extra hurdles than most of their peers, but they can be just as successful."*

Mrs. Sanchez reported that looking at data is essential for the academic performance of migrant students, but she explained that it is most important to look at where they started off when they entered the classroom and how they grew throughout their stay.

"It may take extra time for them to reach their grade level, but with the structure and fidelity and resources, they can attain it."

Data tracking is a significant part of working with migrant students, especially since their stays in a particular classroom may be brief. For teachers assessing levels of achievement, setting goals and tracking them closely is a best practice. When a migrant student leaves, the data will support the efforts of both the teacher and the student. Regardless of what school lies next in their future, they will see themselves as learners and be stronger students because of it.

Identify Learning Gaps and Teach to Them

All of the teachers interviewed were highly familiar with the misalignment of academic standards and expectations across the country. They understood that there is no established system in place to track their proficiencies from state to state. This makes it the teacher's responsibility to pinpoint where the learning gaps are and strategically work towards linking them. Mr. Bodisson maintained that:

"For academic achievement of migrant students it is necessary to find the gap, to find the strategies that will help these students to bridge

the gap, but also to meet their learning styles at the same time."

Time with migrant students is often limited. Identifying gaps can be accomplished formally or informally, however, it must be accomplished in a timely manner. Mr. Gonzalez reported that within his migrant center, progress monitoring happens often.

"We meet as a staff weekly to discuss the lower-level students. We get feedback from classroom teachers and decide where to provide additional help."

The teachers concurred that once the learning gaps are identified, the work to move forward must be strategic, purposeful, and swift. Students can move in and out of a school without warning, so preparing them for wherever they end up is the charge of each of their teachers.

Each of the student participants stated their migrant status caused them to continuously trail their non-migrant peers academically. Hindering their performance either initially or consistently was leaving school a couple of months early, starting school a couple of months late, language barriers, and an array of social weaknesses.

Mateo recalled being retained one year because his parent's migrating pattern did not allow him to attend a mandated summer school session. He explained that most migrant students flunk out because they are unable to monitor themselves.

"As a younger student, I needed teachers who knew what I needed and worked to strengthen my deficits. The grit and the work ethic is already there, but it is only with the proper guidance that I was able to see myself as competent enough to push forward."

Carmen considered herself lucky to have had a teacher take her under her wing and not only educate her but motivate her:

"She would meet with me once a week, just her and I. It was very impactful, especially when she began to push me to apply for college. I struggled in high school and I was ready for graduation because I didn't want to continue struggling. The extra support and words of encouragement is what eventually changed my mindset."

Javier argued that the best teachers in his experience were those that knew how and were committed to handling the stress and challenges that come with instructing students who are failing for reasons beyond their control. He did best in classes where the teachers did not allow him to feel intimidated and provided individualized support every step of the way.

"Not being treated as a seasonal or temporary student, but more as a real and capable student

who could do the work if just given the chance is what made me feel confident."

Carmen remembered being segregated into sheltered type classrooms while in elementary and middle school. She did not like being placed solely with other ELLs who were behind due to their migrant situations.

"Being pulled-out of our regular classrooms to teach us English only put us further behind the other students who were learning new math skills and science. Being isolated only made us feel irrelevant."

Student participant, Luciano, who identified Mrs. Rickard as a model teacher of migrant students, is aligned in theory with the importance of customizing instruction for more meaningful results.

"I did my best learning in Mrs. Rickard's class because she always stopped to make sure that I was getting it. I remember lots and lots of review and practice in her class, because she wouldn't move on until she was satisfied with the learning. I learned so much from her. She was nice, she went out of her way and I respect her for that."

Mr. Bodisson strongly supported the need to supplement instruction in order to teach explicit standards and skills.

"Every migrant student is different and it is up to the teacher to find what strategies are needed."

Bodisson understood the desire to group migrant ELLs together so that they can support each other and collectively translate the instruction, however, he assesses this practice as a limitation to enhancing the learning

"The problem with grouping students by their language and not their academic ability is that teachers teach to the lowest and many students will progress at a slower pace. When they are placed into more mainstream classrooms they are able to progress faster."

Relative to tailoring the instruction for migrant students, Mrs. Rickard contended that differentiation is critical when best supporting migrant students:

"I think that it must be extremely difficult and confusing for students to attend multiple schools in different districts each year. Schools may teach the curriculum in a different order causing students to miss sections or repeating the same sections. Teachers may not be willing to work with students who need different things, because it is definitely additional work. Migrant students need teachers who will figure out the gaps in

knowledge and be willing to do the extra work to help them close the gaps."

Chapter Seven

Theme Three: Experiences that Motivate Gains and Celebrate Milestones are Essential to Success

Intrinsic/Extrinsic rewards are necessary

Most people appreciate being rewarded for their efforts, and migrant students are no different. The one variable, however, is that such rewards for them must be meaningful and consistent. Their seasonal stays in a particular geographical area creates feelings of apprehension and uncertainty. Rewards for meeting a goal or mastering a skill can be intricate in balancing the pressures of their home lives. Maricela recalled sleeping outside at the farmer's market each day waiting for school to start. A reward at school would wake her from her sluggish state and spark her to press forward. Like Maricela, Rigoberto remembered having trouble staying awake in class after working long hours in the fields on weekends or in the packing house in the evenings:

> *"Getting up and going to school was always a struggle, but once I was there my teachers had a way of making me feel alert. My favorite teacher was extra encouraging and really pushed me to do well. I still have all of my certificates that I earned in his class."*

Tomàs joked that his reward for going to school was the air-conditioning, because he had none at home or in the tomato fields.

> *"I never wanted to let my parents down because I knew that while I was in school, they were sacrificing, giving their sweat and tears to provide for us."*

College Visits and Prep Beyond High School Is Paramount

Several of the students I interviewed described having participated in college visits through their high school's migrant center. They collectively identified this experience as principal in helping them make the ultimate decision to further their education beyond high school. Rosalinda had the opportunity to visit several colleges while a junior in high school. Spending time on college campuses allowed her to get a firsthand look at her prospects and helped her to realize that the opportunity for her to attend was no longer far-fetched.

> *"I remember seeing other students on college campuses that looked like me. Visiting colleges was what I think motivated me to keep going."*

Other students credited teachers and guidance counselors who helped them complete college acceptance applications and for best preparing them for the college lifestyle. For Javier, it was an art scholarship that allowed him to chase his college dream. He acknowledged that without support and directions on applying for it, it would have never happened. Luciano remembered the teachers who constantly spoke about the option of attending college.

> *"Just hearing over and over that I was college material made me eventually believe it."*

Carmen's speech pathologist constantly reminded her about the importance of attending college.

> *"I only saw her once a week, but every time I met with her, she talked to me about attending college."*

PREPARE THEM AND HELP THEM TO PLAN FOR THEIR FUTURES

The majority of students interviewed thought that high school best prepared them for college not only academically but socially. With the appropriate resources and support they gain the self-confidence and capabilities to pursue a higher education. Margarita never forgot her high school assistant principal who took her under his wing and did all that he could to ensure that she was college ready.

> *"He taught me to have grit so that I would never be deterred. I still use his lessons in my career today."*

FREQUENT PRAISE IS KEY

Teachers interviewed understood that self-esteem can be an issue for migrant students dealing with the pressures of poverty and insecurity. They understand that parents of migrant students are often uneducated and overwhelmed and have little time or money to reward their children for doing well in school. Praising migrant students is vital to their success as a student, especially when the praise may not be happening at home. Mrs. Rickard expanded,

> *"In my experience, migrant parents do the best that they can for their children. Every child is unique and deserves a teacher who sees him or*

her as a worthy candidate for education. They need to hear that they can do it."

Mrs. Sanchez explained that migrant parents often need to prioritize and don't always put education at the top:

"Some parents need their children to help at home with caring for siblings and chores. School is important to them, but sometimes it has to take a back seat in order to meet the demands of their home life. As teachers, we have to be diligent in our praise and continue to build up their self-esteem."

Each of the students interviewed communicated the power of the relentless praise and celebration delivered by teachers who were key in their survival as students. From sincere words of encouragement to positive and meaningful feedback, these actions to them were unquantifiable. Others recalled unique experiences that pushed them to strive and prevail. Rigoberto said he will never forget the exclusive opportunity to attend a young author's conference and visit with award-winning authors as an experience. It was an incentive for his efforts in writing, and he admitted it was one of the main reasons that he worked so hard to improve his writing.

"It was extra hard for me to earn this reward, but it was worth all the work that I put into it. I am still not the best writer, but I will always remember this trip because it made my whole

family proud and I got to celebrate with people from all over who liked writing."

Estella detailed her motivation as one developed on behalf of her parents.

"I constantly felt like my success was paying back my parents for all of their sacrifices. The field work that they performed involved long, hot, tiring days and my hard work was motivated by their determination for me to finish school."

For Federico, his motivation came from his peers. Regardless of the school that he was attending on any given year, his math skill impressed teachers and students alike. When his peers asked for help and he was able to do so his self-esteem heightened and it helped to make him feel as a fixture in the classroom, rather than the brown-skinned imbecile, who was still building his English vocabulary and who came to school with untamed hair and hand-me-down clothes.

"When my teachers saw how strong my math skills were and they let me help my classmates when they were stuck, I felt like I belonged. I was happy to help and it gave me a sense of worth. At home, things were different because my parents worked such long hours. I had to help with my

brothers and sisters and that was never a choice, it was what I had to do."

A high school guidance counselor who continues to support migrant students, Mrs. Garza said many migrant students are self-motivated because of their migrant lifestyle. Recognizing that education is the one factor that can pull them out of the cycle of poverty, she explained that their drive comes from their daily experiences.

"We have some migrant students at our school doing incredible things, sometimes outperforming their non-migrant peers. Because of their migrant lifestyle, which may include going hungry, trouble sleeping and sharing a home with another family, they are driven to do all that they can to one day live without having to struggle."

Mrs. Garza added that most of the migrant students that she has had the pleasure of working with have big dreams and a strong will.

"They are competent and capable of doing anything that they set their mind to, but we have to give them the required attention that they deserve."

Mrs. Sanchez held the same position, supporting the need to guide, influence and activate enthusiasm.

"Students coming into this country are hungrier for success. A migrant family's struggles can help fuel them, making them hunger for more. I've never shied away from giving my students hugs and telling them I love them, that I believed in them and that I wanted them to do well."

Sanchez asserted that many of the tactics that she uses with her migrant students are just standard best practices; however, she said she sometimes goes above and beyond to let them know how important they are:

"I have attended their sporting events and birthday parties. If there was a student that was falling through the cracks, and I understood their home struggles, I found ways to reach them by either inviting them out to eat, or to the movies. Sometimes these outings were beyond my teaching salary, but they were essential to building lasting relationships and a love of learning"

Chapter Eight

Theme Four: Using All Resources Available, Including Parent Involvement, is Key!

Supplies and tutors help to level the equity

M igrant farm work does not involve great wages. Migrant students come to school with few resources and are appreciative of any supplies made available to them. Having the necessary supplies for learning, no doubt, helps to level the playing field and assists migrant students to feel prepared for the already challenging job of learning. Estella recalled getting supplies from her school's migrant center.

"Getting a backpack filled with school supplies took the pressure off of my mom having to buy them for me. Having the right supplies, I had no excuse for not trying my best in class."

Estella also was grateful for the personnel in her school's migrant center for helping her study for tests and editing her writing assignments.

"I didn't have the advantage of going home and having my mom help me with my homework. Having people in place to take on this role saved me."

Rosalinda recalled a program that gave backpacks and supplies to her at the start of each school year.

"Without these donations, I would have not even wanted to go to school. I would have felt awkward."

USE ALL RESOURCES AVAILABLE

Several of the students interviewed indicated that, without the additional resources provided specifically for them, high school graduation would not have been possible. For most, the support in the form of supplies, technology, and tutoring was a luxury. Amancia explained that while her parents tried to help, she often had to seek out help from school:

"I am glad that there were programs and people willing to help me out when my parents couldn't. No one in my family had ever gone to college, so I didn't even know where to start, how to apply for scholarships or financial aid."

Federico noted that he initially did not want to use his school's migrant center to ask for help, because he thought he would be made fun of. But he was relieved when he finally went in to ask for help.

"I didn't want to go in there because I thought it was only for students who couldn't speak English. When I learned that I could use their computers, I was in there every day afterschool. It was a resource that I really came to appreciate."

Communicate with Parents Regularly

Teachers often find that communicating with parents is a challenge. When attempting to contact the parents of migrant students, the challenge is multiplied. Many of their parents speak no English, lack cellphones, and are unreachable while they are out working in the fields. The teachers interviewed attest to the challenge but kept trying so that parents knew about their child's advancements. Mr. Wells commented,

"They often do not understand the ability that their kids may have and as a result have very different goals for them."

Mrs. Sanchez acknowledged it can be unfair to ask parents of migrant students to come in for conferences do to their work schedules. She used notes home and evening phone calls to make contact:

"Migrant parents cannot just leave work and come in for a meeting. They count on every hour of work. Sometimes if it rains and they are unable to go to work, you might be able to connect with them. For the most part, you have to be willing to make time to meet with them on their schedules. Yes, it can be difficult but there are a lot of rewards in keeping them informed."

Educate parents about student capabilities and opportunities

Teachers interviewed understood that parents of migrant students want what is best for them. Their differences in culture sometimes causes them to step back and not ask questions. Their respect for teachers as professionals is profound. While they will often not stop by the school or call to check on the status of their child, they are always grateful to hear from their teachers. Mr. Gonzalez explained that developing great relationships with the families of migrant students is just as important as the one developed with the student.

"The parental piece is important. If they are informed they will be our allies. They come to this country for the opportunity it offers and for a better life. They encourage their children to take advantage of the education system and do well in school."

Mrs. Sanchez added that involving and educating the parents is always beneficial. She said learning from her students and families was "paramount":

"We [want to] educate the whole child and empower them with the tools to become productive. When the parents of migrant students hear what their child can do and learns about the opportunities available to them, they will do whatever they can to provide support."

Eleven of the 12 former migrant students who took part in this study graduated from the same high school. The school is located in a rural agricultural community with a third of the student body identified as migrant. As a result, the district provides a migrant resource center that is housed within the school. Offering a computer lab, tutoring, and consumable resources such as school supplies and backpacks, this support is not seen in most school settings. Javier's experience with the school's migrant center helped him in his transition into college, even providing him and interested classmates with tours of local colleges and assistance in filling out scholarship applications.

> *"These resources were not available in other schools that I attended and it was a great way to make sure that I was knowledgeable about what was out there. The center also helped me out when I was in a bind or needed extra help."*

Amancia said getting to know the needs of the migrant students and then ensuring that they have the resources to succeed is a required combination.

> *"You have to provide them with the resources, even if that means showing them where to go and helping them get there. We are not all confident and self-sufficient. As much as we want to do well, we sometimes don't have the skills to ask for support."*

For Amancia, the resources continued at the college level. It was through her high school's migrant center that she learned about the College Assistance Migrant Program at Michigan State University. The two programs worked collectively to ensure a smooth stress-free transition, even considering the change in climate.

> *"Living in Florida, I was used to the heat. I had never even seen snow until I began attending*

MSU. The cold weather was unbearable, but the CAMP program went as far as making sure that I had an appropriate coat and shoes for the snow. They were not giving me an excuse to give up."

Tomàs recognized his high school's migrant center as impactful and influential. He describes the personnel assigned to the center as understanding and empathetic from the perspective of the students that they served.

"The extra resources and the extra pushes that they gave me were always appreciated. The center always made you feel welcomed which made it easier to ask for a pack of paper or help with an assignment."

Mr. Gonzalez, who now manages his school's migrant center, echoed the need to provide applicable resources in a reverential manner.

"We must have high expectations for our students, we have to respect their lifestyle and guide them towards using the resources available to them. Our students who start school up north and then join us when the fieldwork up there is done, all say the same thing. They feel like our school is their home, because this is where resources are provided and this is where they feel the most comfortable going to school."

Mr. Gonzalez added that the relationships are just as strong with the student's families, often including them in the ins and outs of their child's progress, struggles and breakthroughs.

> *"If the parents are on board, it makes it so much easier for our migrant students to achieve success."*

This unique migrant center is a hub of Immokalee High School and serves an average of 80 to 100 students each school day. Whether students come in for supplies or for academic support, the services are tracked and used to assess the benefits of the center. Their data are evaluated and correlated to the school's graduation rate, the amount of migrant students who continue their education after high school and the amount of CAMP programs visiting the school to recruit students. The most compelling evidence, however, as cited by Mr. Gonzalez, is when the students come back after graduation to thank the staff members for the help they provided.

Mrs. Rickard explained that migrant resources are critical because most migrant students do not have the parental support to supplement the imparities:

> *"Migrant parents do the best that they can for their children, but many have limited educations themselves and are not able to help their students as much as they would like. When schools support parents and give them tools to help their children, most of the parents are grateful and will implement the tools at home."*

Rickard justified the need to fully understand and support migrant students in order to lead them to success.

"Adequate school support including teachers, including support staff and parental support are required factors. Schools that address the need of the entire child and do not just focus on the academic piece will have more successful migrant students."

While Mr. Bodisson believed that migrant parents want to be a resource for their children, he understands that they are limited in their abilities to help.

"Migrant parents know more than anyone the struggles of a lack of education and opportunity and the impact it can have on their future."

Mr. Wells suggested that

"migrant students and their parents deal with problems that their non-migrant peers will never have to deal with."

This added burden obliges schools to provide resources which will help to even the playing field. Mrs. Sanchez attests that when all available resources are utilized, the results are the most encouraging.

"Academic achievement for migrant students is not a far-fetched goal with the proper parental support, suitable resources, strong and structured classrooms and of course the drive that the students themselves bring with them. When all of these structures are in place and present, any migrant student can succeed."

This mindset for Mrs. Sanchez is what she feels sets migrant students up for success. As she saw it, matching quality instructors with available resources and ensuring that their parents are in the loop are equally important.

Chapter Nine

A Summary of the Themes: A Bundle for Success

With the population of migrant students on the increase in classrooms across the country, it is necessary for teachers to better understand their situations and identify practices that will best support them academically. The purpose of this study was to isolate the best approaches as recognized by former migrant students themselves who had gained success as college graduates. Coupled with their indicators for best results were the shared dogmas of their former teachers who had been characterized as influential by their former students.

With the focus of identifying best practices for successfully working with migrant students, the findings revealed that because this group comes with unique needs and experiences, it is important to approach them with unique and sometimes individualized methodologies. Much of the literature indicated that multiple factors must be addressed when meeting the academic needs of migrant students. Such factors include equity pedagogy, cultural respect, inclusivity, language, and access to resources.

The student participants and the teachers of migrant students agreed that treating migrant students as permanent students versus temporary students is the first step in establishing an equity pedagogy. Equity pedagogy refers to "teaching strategies and classroom environments that help students from diverse groups attain the knowledge and skills needed to function effective while creating a just, humane and democratic society" (Banks & Banks, 1995, p. 152). It speaks to treating all students equally with reverence and value. As a result of coming to school weeks or months later than most of their peers, migrant students come with social anxieties that are only multiplied when teachers make them feel like outsiders. Feeling included and accepted as an equal is critical for thriving as a migrant student when friendships and relationships are often cut short.

The first theme isolated from the interviews is relative to working to understand the migrant student's lifestyle. The students affirmed that when a teacher takes the extra time to get to know them and learn about their migrating experiences, family life, and travels, a special rapport is developed that can lead to an authentic teacher/student relationship. The teacher participants noted that when energies are put into building meaningful rapports with their migrant students, they open up, become participatory, and are able to feel worthy as a learner. Building strong connections is fundamental to all positive teacher/student relationships; however, migrant students require reliable and authenticated interactions that are frequent and specific. Every involvement in each school and classroom that they attend, while temporary in nature, becomes a permanent part of their everlasting identity.

The second theme addresses the need to provide individualized and supplemental instruction in order to close the many learning gaps. Both groups of participants suggested learning gaps are inevitable and commonplace with migrant students. Regardless of how much a migrant student wants to succeed, the learning gaps that result from transferring from school to school and state to state is expected. The teacher participants explained that with varying standards and expectations across the country, learning for migrants is never seamless. Depending on where, geographically, a student begins or ends the school year, learning loss is foreseeable. These learning gaps, if left unaddressed, will compound over time and increase in severity, potentially forcing students to drop out of school.

The students revered teachers who took measures to fill the learning gaps through individualized and targeted support. While most migrant students who travel across state lines may bring school records such as grades and test scores with them, they do not best reveal where a student is academically and they do not always mesh between school districts and states. Thus, steadfast teachers are forced to identify promptly any gaps and to work strategically to provide remediation. The students credited these efforts as critical to their overall success. The teachers understood that ignoring the need to assess and remediate accordingly would only work against them and impede their own success as teachers.

The third theme, also discussed by both groups of participants, was the benefit of providing experiences that motivate gains and celebrating milestones. For the migrant students who often felt out of place or not up to par with their non-migrant counterparts, being commended for specific achievements or triumphs did wonders for their self-esteem. Several students recalled how profound the earning of certificates or awards for reaching certain goals was. Having these certificates with them as they migrated to foreign schools in faraway states served as reminders of their potential. Motivation and incentives are what drive students to continue reaching and setting new goals. For those students interviewed, constant praise is indispensable as it acts as a driving force to combat the overwhelming struggles of the migrant lifestyle.

The teacher participants established that guiding and witnessing students grow and accomplish goals is the main reason that they went into education. For them, understanding that all students need motivation is fundamental to teaching. Simultaneously, these same teachers recognize that celebrating accomplishments leads to enhanced self-confidence. These teachers understand that migrant students often lack self-assurance and the need to heighten the applause and celebration is constructive and compulsory. They communicated a mutual understanding of the benefits of sending home awards and words of praise in their native language and ensuring that a phone call to their parent is made to include them in the celebration.

The fourth theme that emerged from both participating groups was the importance of utilizing all resources available, including parental involvement. All but one of the students interviewed graduated from the same high school. That school has housed a migrant center for numerous year which each of the students confirmed utilizing. Collectively, the students saw the migrant center as a contributing component of their academic victories. Noting that the center provided resources that they would have ultimately had to do without, each of them expressed gratitude for the availability of consumable supplies, technology and trained personnel.

The availability of meaningful resources is something most teachers never take for granted. Four of the six teachers interviewed worked on the same campus as the student participants. Having others to collaborate with and who understand the importance of equalizing the playing field through essential resources was vital to their success as teachers. Each of the teachers asserted that parental support is just as vital. The teachers said it was vital to conduct home visits, conferences in the parents' native language, and invite parents in to discuss challenges and achievements. The teachers believed acknowledging that effective work with migrant students cannot be accomplished in isolation, suggesting the task of educating migrant students is an intricate one that requires all stakeholders, along with their distinctive resources, to merge purposefully for prime results.

DISCUSSION OF THE RESULTS

To answer the research question at hand, it was necessary to interview those who had a first-hand experience with successful approaches and were positively impacted: former migrant students who excelled and went on to earn college degrees. In order to best corroborate their testimonials, it was important to interview those who provided the approaches: teachers of migrant students. Both sets of interviews suggested that success with migrant students relies on four themes: working to understand the migrant student lifestyle is necessary, individualized and supplemental instruction works to close learning gaps, experiences that motivate gains and celebrate milestones are essential to success, and utilizing all resources available, including parental involvement, is key.

While each migrant student had a distinctive story, many parallels were revealed. Regardless of what states they migrated to or how much school that each of them missed, the commonalities amongst what aided them academically were evident. None of the students saw the need for lowered expectations. Instead, they complimented those teachers who kept the expectations high, but understood that their migrant lifestyle called for understanding and patience. Being seen at times as "temporary students" did not support the trust-building that is required for students who have little opportunities to make connections before packing up and moving on to their next school. Their most favorable teachers were those who took the time not only to understand them but to understand their learning gaps, identify them, and incorporate methodologies to remediate.

Theme One: The Need to Understand the Migrant Student Lifestyle

As the first theme of this study, it was determined that it was essential to understand the migrant student lifestyle. Both student and teacher participants distinguished this premise of an accurate understanding as fundamental to building a relationship that would foster learning. Because the lifestyle of a migrant family is so unusual, it is often difficult for teachers to empathize with this type of student. Instability and change bring result in students' sense of not belonging and anxiety, which most teachers are not prepared to deal with. Student Tomàs recalled the positive ways in which certain teachers would interact with him to help him feel secure and relaxed. "When you feel liked and worthy," he explained, "it makes you feel special and it makes you want to learn." Others referred to the need for compassion and consideration as vital to making them sense that they were just as significant as their non-migrant classmates.

The teachers concurred that meeting the social/emotional needs of each one of their students is what good teachers do. They also agreed that the need to get to know their migrant students at a deeper and more delicate level is a prerequisite to their learning process. "Most migrant students come equipped with high academic capabilities," noted Mrs. Garza. "Once they feel valued and not part of the minority their insecurities seem to disappear." Other teachers interviewed echoed her sentiments, maintaining that migrant students are fragile due to their experiences with poverty, language, and uncertainty as mobile learners. The contention that migrant students will always incur learning gaps was highly disputed by those same teachers, asserting that the learning will happen when the conditions are emboldening and nurturing.

THEME TWO: INDIVIDUALIZED AND SUPPLEMENTAL INSTRUCTION WORKS TO CLOSE LEARNING GAPS

Migrant students who miss numerous days of school each year to follow the harvest of crops with their families endure gaps in their learning. Traveling across state lines where the curriculum standards and expectations vary only widens the gaps. Interviews with both the students and the teachers confirmed this common concern. Both groups acknowledged that the learning gaps can be overwhelming and are generally out of their control. The students interviewed revered those teachers who used their professional expertise to do what they could to hone in on missed skills and bridge students' learning. Respectful teachers who saw students' potential and did not discriminate against them as a result of their limitations are now revered as their best advocates.

The teachers confirmed that relying on deliberate individualized and supplemental instruction led to success in decreasing learning gaps among their migrant students. The result included producing accomplished, self-reliant migrant students who were equipped with the requisite proficiencies to further their education. The formula that each teacher used varied dependent on the needs of each student; however, each teacher described protocols that required investments of added time and energy. Two of the teachers interviewed discussed providing before and after-school support, while the other four detailed using their school's migrant center and its resources. The resources identified included communicating with parents via the home/school liaison, technology programs for practice, and mentoring.

Theme Three: Experiences That Motivate Gains and Celebrate Milestones Are Essential to Success

The semi-structured interviews also revealed the critical need for providing experiences that motivate gains and celebrating milestones with all migrant students. The students noted the array of benefits that come from positive praise and timely, genuine recognitions. They collectively described feeling lost or ill-equipped upon entering a new classroom late in the school year. When their teachers made them feel accomplished and adept and celebrated their progress, it drove the students to strive for added gains, minimizing their initial feelings of distress. Rosalinda told of how proud the recognitions made her and how it in turn helped her to cease constantly doubting herself. Tom remembered how he relished in challenges and competitions that required him to set goals and work diligently to meet them. His success in earning points and certificates for passing reading quizzes motivated him to press forward. Several of the students interviewed credited positive praise and celebrations for helping to offset their anxieties and building their confidence. Changing their mindset about their intelligence and abilities was seen as necessary in order to combat their feelings of constant defeat as they travelled from school to school amid continuous shifting.

Even though teachers are thoroughly trained to make learning fun and celebrate milestones, the teachers interviewed distinguished this as a nonnegotiable when working with migrant students. Understanding their lifestyle and the long-term stress that can come with it, they saw it vital to offer constant praise and intentional opportunities to celebrate. Mrs. Sanchez declared that migrant students are often not praised at home because of the workload or lack of skills from the parents, which can stifle their children's learning. The teachers agreed that migrant students come to school without a strong emotional base, and working to strengthen it should be a priority. Bringing joy and excitement into their lives, even if only during the school day, can be crucial in developing standards for living well, which include celebrating successes, establishing self-assurance, and recognizing potentials.

Theme Four: Utilizing All Resources Available, Including Parental Involvement, Is Key

The final theme identified addressed the importance of utilizing all resources available, including parental involvement. All but one of the student participants had the amenity of attending and graduating from a high school that was equipped with a staffed migrant center, which supported the students from the time they arrived at the school until graduation. For several students, it helped support them beyond high school graduation, serving as a link between high school and college assistance migrant programs. The students each utilized the migrant center at varying regularities depending on their needs, for example, to secure basic supplies, use technology, and receive supplemental instruction from trained staff. The students described the level of engagement with the migrant center personnel as inviting and intimate. Working to make connections with their families to communicate progress aided in alleviating the feelings of burden that comes from living in poverty. Those who attended schools in other states for brief periods were reminded of the luxury of having a migrant center. When such resources are not available to students, they slide academically and require additional support upon their return to their home school.

The teachers interviewed indicated that all migrant students need such resources, but they knew that their school was atypical. Three of the teacher participants shared that they were indebted to the migrant center housed at their campus. They agreed that the resources have to be wanted rather than forced, noting a strong correlation between a skilled teacher who motivates students to seek extra outside support that is compassionate and accommodating. All teachers said migrant parents need to be involved in their children's education. Communicating academic standings, gains, and strengths to them in their native language allowed them to take important information with them in their travels. Additionally, the teachers described the advantages of empowering parents of migrant students so that they are better equipped to support them in their endeavors beyond high school. The final step in releasing the students to post high school ventures was informing parents about the opportunities available to their children and guiding them along the way to their children's college education.

Chapter Ten

CONNECTIONS TO THE RESEARCH

The current literature related to best practices for teachers of migrant students to utilize for optimal success centered mostly on providing students with a nurturing, empathetic, and committed approach. Although past research is limited and inconclusive, the literature has suggested that migrant students seem to perform stronger when the opportunities to do so are sincere, personalized, and focused. Participants in this study provided distinctive insight into the methodologies necessary to best educate migrant students. The experiences of each of the participants will supplement the available literature while simultaneously providing insight for current and future teachers of migrant students and researchers. Within the literature review, it was gathered that effective teachers of migrant students must work extra hard to bring about positive results. Much of the research also gave credence to the importance of the need to be inclusive of the migrant student culture. Additionally, school leaders need to find additional funding and access to better support for migrant students.

Araujo (2012) observed that the work migrant families do is strenuous and that their travels only add to the stress. He added that the struggles become intense for migrant students as they attempt to infuse themselves into unfamiliar campuses. The students interviewed spoke about their struggles and substantiated the anxiety that comes when having to relocate and enter a new school. They shared the excitement of returning to their "home base," where they spent the greater part of their school year and eventually graduated. The familiar campus with recognizable teachers brought them a sense of stability, even if only short-lived. The student participants echoed that the variances in learning standards and expectations made for much of the apprehension. Regardless of their capabilities, the learning gaps which were beyond their control often made them appear to be incompetent and unqualified to learn.

The teachers interviewed who had been successful in working with migrant students echoed the need to understand the struggle of the migrant family. The teachers revealed that they had to approach their migrant students with caution because of the unique strains that moving and adapting to new situations can put on a child. Free (2016) argued that, as a result of their transient and unstable lifestyle, feelings of fear and temporary existence can negatively impact students' education. The teachers asserted that upon understanding what students endure in order to survive, an effective and caring teacher will work to remove the fears and bring about a sense of belonging. Relative to feelings of non-belonging, migrant students report high rates of stigmatization, distrust of authority figures, and feeling of anxiety, frustration, and dreading the future (Sulkowski, 2017). Maslow (as cited in McLeod, 2017) acknowledged that human motivation is based on an individual's needs being met. Ensuring that children's basic needs are met is vital in all classrooms. The teachers interviewed shared educational philosophies grounded in Maslow's theory and saw it as imperative, especially in children of poverty and where English is a second language.

Teachers must also determine where to begin with instruction with respect to their children's learning gaps. Irizarry and Williams (2013) cited research suggesting that migrant children, because of their academic lags, require more than typical delivery of curriculum. The teachers I interviewed suggested they had to identify learning gaps and implement strategic methods to guide students to close those gaps while bridging them with new or common skills.

This research was designed to discover effective approaches to best support migrant students educationally. As the diversity of migrant population continues to grow, systems to support them educationally must be prepared to support the best practices for optimal results (Grisham-Brown & McCormick, 2013). The teacher participants stated that being successful with their migrant students always required extra efforts beyond the school day, and that training and support is essential for teachers struggling to make gains with this unique population.

The students acknowledged their own prior learning gaps and told of their frustration when the learning was either repeated or unconnected to prior schooling. As young students they did not understand that the gaps were beyond their control, and as a result they developed stigmas that decreased their motivation. Irizarry and Williams (2013) noted that support for migrant students with learning gaps requires more than foundational skills and grade-level content expectations. Explaining to students the cause of their academic lags, rather than allowing them to believe that they are incapable, could have saved them from unnecessary anxiety. Romanowski (2003) supported this idea, contending that obstacles to the success of migrant students stem from teachers' lack of understanding of their own beliefs about migrant students, which are influenced by prejudices that guide their behavior and actions.

Banks (1993) argued teachers must resist seeing multicultural education as merely content integration; rather, it should be viewed as a restructuring that allows all students to acquire knowledge, attitudes, and skills required to function with success in a diverse world. The migrant students I interviewed revealed positive experiences in which the teachers used their unique travelling experiences and backgrounds to help make connections, build trust, and bring them in as bona fide contributors to their classroom. This notion supports Kugler (2018), who suggested schools must shift their focus from using high-stakes testing and fact drilling to narrow the achievement gap and build a culture that supports the ideology that every student from every background has value. Each one of the student participants cited respectful teachers who treated them as learners with potential as a major contributor to their success.

The resources available to the student participants proved to be not only powerful but greatly appreciated. While past research has focused on summer migrant education programs rather than the on campus migrant center experienced by the participating students, their purpose for helping migrant students "catch up" are identical. The students consider themselves lucky to have attended a high school campus that provided the migrant center as a resource. Unfortunately, such programs are limited in both location and funding. Torrez (2014) asserted that without proper funding, support, or resources, attempts to take migrant students to advanced levels of education will fail to support them in realizing their potential.

Consequently, the teacher participants expressed a great deal of gratitude for the migrant resources and support that they have been allotted. Confirming that the task of best educating a migrant student requires a team of compassionate and skilled professionals, the teachers understood that schools where some of their students came from may not have had the added resources. Virta (2014) explained that despite the success of these support systems, the added staff can be costly and difficult to find and schedule, especially in school where migrant populations are limited. The students maintained the value of the migrant center and described a contrast to their learning when enrolled at other schools that did not provide them with similar resources.

Chapter Eleven

THE MIGRANT AUTHOR: CONNECTIONS TO SELF, EVERY MIGRANT MILE OF THE WAY

As a fellow former Migrant student, the pages of this publication bring back countless inimitable memories, some encouraging, some woeful, but all promising, especially for those presently toiling through the process. The journey for children, while filled with miles of exciting memories and day-to-day surprises, can similarly be gloomy, literally filthy and often unreliable. Today, allocations in funding help school districts provide necessary support, but when the support is temporary and with an unpredictable timetable, so much is lost in transition, in translation, leaving unfilled learning gaps that fail to mesh from state to state.

I like to consider myself one of the "lucky ones." Growing up, when migrant season began, my dad would make the northbound trip on his own, coming back for us as soon as the school year ended. Without fail, the last day of school consisted of classroom parties celebrating the end of another school year followed by an evening of packing, loading up the truck and prepping the house for a summer of absence. The day after the last day of school, the northern trek began. Situated in the bed of my dad's pickup truck that was carefully loaded on the back of a large flatbed field truck, the trip itself was thrilling. I spent much of the two days reading and napping, trying not to think about the fieldwork that laid ahead. The work would be wearisome, the temperatures would be unbearable, but it was what we did.

Once the workdays came into full effect, my luck felt as if it had come to a screeching halt and the long days of backbreaking labor matured my thoughts almost immediately. This was hard work, some days the sun shone at over one-hundred degrees. Nevertheless, alongside my parents and sisters, the harvest was at the top of our to-do list, so we pushed forward. After lunch was always the worst, hot and humid with no clouds in sight. With tears dripping down my face, I vowed to break this cycle. Neither of my parents had more than a sixth-grade education, and they used these dreadful experiences to open our eyes to what could be. As noble as this work was, I knew that it wasn't for me.

Numerous comparable summers followed. Each one had me closer to graduation, gung-ho at never returning, never looking back. The annual ten weeks in Michigan or the Carolina's were memorable, no doubt. Staying in dilapidated homes, built decades before with old plumbing and faulty wiring, sleeping in squeaky beds framed out of wrought iron, squeaky used mattresses and walking on just as squeaky natural wooden floors, not always in the best condition, were each daily reminders that we were disadvantaged. Despite it being the early 80s it was a 1950s vibe with matching appliances, furniture and aesthetics, far from fancy, far from ordinary, far from home.

My favorite part of these temporary quarters was the picturesque front porch, which was customary on such homes. It was here where we put on our socks and shoes amid the rising sun each morning as we got ready for work. It was here that we sat and took them off after a log day of fieldwork, the smell of heavy labor as we swatted them against the edges of the wooden slabs that lined the steps. If there was time before nightfall, the porch served as a play area. Card and board games is what we played, our bodies too sore for skipping and jumping.

Fields of corn, tobacco or cucumbers usually surrounded the property. All perfect venues for rounds and rounds of hide-and-seek. This was our week-end fun, or on those rainy days when picking was cancelled. Ventures to the local parks and tourist sites often filled our weekends, but only if we fulfilled the work goals for the week that dad has established. Fieldwork, didn't wait for weekends and still doesn't. Only Mother Nature would give us days off.

Now, working in a school with a high migrant population, I love to ask our incoming students about the places that they are coming from. Probing about the weather and their former housing always brings back memories. As the Media Specialist, I am charged with issuing laptops to all students on their first day of school and collecting them on their last.

As a result, I have the delight of meeting our newest migrant students and helping to make them feel at home and the pleasure of wishing them well on their last day as they undertake an unpredictable prospect. Having first hand knowledge of the trepidations that come with being a migrant student, I am never short in putting myself out as an anchor of support.

As a teacher of migrant students, my background enabled me to provide these students with exactly what they needed. Being cognizant of all of the questions and qualms that they had gave me an advantage as I worked to bring them in and allow the new learning to link to the old, with the understanding that our class was a safe zone. Because migrant teachers with migrant backgrounds are scarce, I knew that spreading what I knew was required. Migrant students have spread incalculably throughout the country. As educators, we owe it to them to understand them. Regardless of how they came across our border, they are here, they are innocent and they deserve the best of what we have to offer. A wise principal once told me that "Parents send us their best children." Teachers who are truly in it for the cause don't dramatize or belittle those with learning and language gaps. They take on the challenge, letting pedagogy be their guide, and engage in fearless days of meaningful experiences.

Migrant students don't require pity, sympathy or unadulterated charity. Like most students, they bode well with self-esteem building, purposeful instruction and a resilient rapport built on trust and respect. Add a few helpings of thoughtful empathy that appreciates cultures and distinct differences, and a robust migrant educator is poised for service. Once the anxiety that comes from trying to communicate in a new language or in a new setting subsides, constructs can come alive and the learning may begin. Steady baby steps will turn in to larger strides and it is here where college success stories are born.

Chapter Twelve

CONCLUSION

C harged with the goal of identifying approaches that best support the learning of migrant students, a key finding consisted of common expectations for meeting student needs and bridging their learning gaps. Understanding the predicament of the migrant lifestyle and making deliberate efforts to provide inviting and well-intended learning environments is crucial. The participants you met in chapter three described the need for equity and the value of taking advantage of resources that can supplement the learning.

Teaching migrant students who experience detrimental learning gaps resulting from their untimely travels can be a challenging task. The disparity in practice is that most teachers do not understand their dilemmas and incorrectly characterize them as inept and unteachable. The teachers interviewed asserted that such students require specialized attention. Two strategic methodologies for changing the course of current practice are building positive student-teacher relationships, which is the moral fiber of multicultural education, and discrediting misconceptions about what migrant students are able to do. Relative to Maslow's principles, understanding that positive and meaningful student-teacher relationships cannot be accomplished without first meeting basic needs is essential.

Implementing the practice recommendations of genuinely considering migrant student needs as a result of their lifestyle, teaching strategically and systematically to bridge learning and fill gaps and providing constant and significant praise will support in increasing the academic performance of migrant students. Focusing on these recommendations, as provided by both teacher and student participants in this study, can profoundly shape the state of migrant education. Providing training for teachers to better understand the plight of the migrant farmworker family could aid in prompting teachers of migrant students to approach them tactfully. The end result could benefit academic improvement.

The hope is that these findings create opportunities for policy makers to establish training protocols for teachers working with migrant students. The migrant student population is booming thus, the need to make these trainings a component of teacher preparation courses is prudent. When all teachers have adequate training to best support and handle any migrant students who are enrolled into their classrooms, they will be better prepared to initiate learning without causing unnecessary friction or discord that could cause the student to withdraw and regress.

A major issue identified with educating migrant students is the delay in learning when they arrive on a new campus. Aligning learning standards from state to state or even district to district could prove effective in alleviating the added time required to access and analyze learning gaps, proficiency levels and mastery of skills. Policies to support the streamlining of transferring such information, whether digitally or on a standardized form, could work to accelerate the transition and save valuable instructional time.

Funding for added resources, such as those provided to and utilized by this study's students, are costly. Policies to enhance funding to best support the needs of migrant students can complement the recommended approaches. Olwig and Valentin (2015) reported that insufficient resources can cause migrant students to be misplaced in classrooms that emasculate their potential. Lack of funding creates an evident absence of equity for this unique population. Banks (2010), through his definition of multicultural education, explained that educational equality will continue to be a barrier for minority students until a focus is placed its importance. Funding policies for migrant education through training, added personnel and resources illustrate the reverence to the "no child left behind" ideology and the commitment to ensuring equal educational opportunities.

Maslow's hierarchy of needs theory coupled with multicultural education served as frameworks for this study. The hierarchy of needs theory is a five-level pyramid in which higher needs come into focus only once basic needs are met (Maslow, as cited in McLeod, 2017). Understanding that migrant students are typically economically disadvantaged, teachers must establish systems to ensure that their most basic needs are met. Issues with hunger, sleep deprivation, and good health are all critical to learning preparedness.

Simultaneously, districts and state and federal legislators must also do their part to fund initiatives. Once these needs are met, their teachers can work to create strong positive relationships. Murray and Malmgren (2005) concluded that low-income students who establish strong relationships with their teachers yield higher academic achievement and have more positive social-emotional adjustments than their peers who do not. In my interviews, migrant students and their teachers all identified encouraging and sincere relationships as fundamental to their success.

Relative to multicultural education, there is a clear paradigm shift in theory that will mandate a mindset that is all-inclusive and strives to create a culture where students are empowered based on their self-worth in learning spaces where everyone is treated with respect and promise. Multicultural education not only improves student productivity but simultaneously helps to overcome prejudices and build interpersonal communication while creating an awareness of culture and preventing social conflicts (Ameny-Dixon, 2013). Equity is deprived when students are treated as "temporary" and overlooked because the assumption of the teachers is that they will leave before any progress can be achieved or measured. Migrant students have a better chance of seeing themselves as potential college graduates when teachers recognize their differences as strengths and quality instruction is provided to all. Migrant students carry their linguistic and cultural richness with them wherever they go. When their teachers fail to recognize their strengths and use them to their advantage, students struggle to adapt (Rodriguez-Valls & Torres, 2014).

The current research on migrant education and the approaches required to best approach migrant students is limited. Although migrant students' success stories have been documented, they are heavily outnumbered by those of migrant students who fall through the cracks, drop-out of school, and cycle through poverty. The research that advises what migrant teachers can and should do is important, but little research has identified what teachers can do to best guide and educate their migrant students. This study was one attempt to fill that gap.

Further research looking into the perspective of school administrators and their mindset on what they perceive as equitable and appropriate for educating migrant students could garner alternate recommendations on how to best attack the issues negatively affecting student success. Most school administrators have experienced the role of the teacher and could provide insight on both instructional needs and policy implementation.

Examining former migrant students who did not enjoy success as students and were unable to break away from the migrant lifestyle could also prove to offer insight that looks closer at the pressures and adverse effects of current practices.

This research serves as an overview of what migrant students expect in school as they travel from state to state with their farmworker families in search of work. Additionally, it provided best practices and insights from teachers who have experienced success in teaching migrant students. Awareness of the complexity of the migrant way of life and the universal ambitions of the migrant student must be understood by all stakeholders in the education field. The findings from this study contribute to the current yet limited research on the topic and can be used to help guide future research. The hope of the author is that results from this study can help support changes in practice, policy, and theory with the goal of enhancing the educational experiences of migrant students so that all students are provided the same level of quality and opportunity.

References

ABC10 News. (2017). Florida teacher reassigned after criticizing "Day Without Immigrants" movement. Retrieved from http://www.10news.com/news/national/naples-teacher-reassigned-afterimmigration-post_

Adelman, H., & Taylor, L. (2015). Immigrant children and youth in the USA: Facilitating equity of opportunity at school. *Education Sciences*, 323–344. Volume 5 https://doi.org/10.3390/educsci5040323

Alsubaie, M. A. (2015). Examples of certain issues in the multicultural classroom. *Journal of Educational Practice,* 6(10) pps 86–89. Retrieved from https://files.eric.ed.gov/fulltext/EJ1081654.pdf

Amankwaa, L. (2016). Creating protocols for trustworthiness in qualitative research. *Journal of Cultural Diversity, 23*(3), 121–127.

Ameny-Dixon, M. G. (2013). *Why multicultural education is important higher education now than ever: A global perspective.* Retrieved from http://www.nationalforum.com/Electronic%20Journal%20Volumes/AmenyDixon,%20Gloria%20M.%20Why%20Multicultural%20Education%20is%20More%20Important%20in%20Higher%20Education%20Now%20than%20Ever.pdf

Amuedo-Dorantes, C., & Antman, F. (2016). Can authorization reduce poverty among undocumented immigrants? Evidence from the Deferred Action for Childhood Arrivals program. *Economics Letters, 146,* 1–4

Araujo, B. (2012). Knowledge from the fields: a migrant farmworker student's community cultural wealth. *Diaspora, Indigenous, and Minority Education,* 6(2), 85–98. Retrieved from http://dx.doi.org/10.1080/15595692.2012.66259

Au, W. (2017). When multicultural education is not enough. *Multicultural Perspectives, 19*(3), 147–150. https://doi.org/10.1080/15210960.2017.1331741

Banks, J. A. (1993a). Multicultural education: Development, dimensions and challenges. *Phi Delta Kappan, 75*(1), 22–28. Retrieved from https://education.uw.edu/sites/default/files/20405019.pdf

Banks, J. A. (1993b). Multicultural education: Historical development, dimensions and practice. *Review of Research in Education, 19,* 3–49.

Banks, J. A. (2010). *Multicultural education: Issues and perspectives* (7th ed.). New York, NY: John Wiley and Sons.

Banks, J. A., & Banks, C. A. M. (Eds.). (2002). *Handbook of research on multicultural education* (2nd ed.). San Francisco, CA: Jossey-Bass.

Baraldi, C. (2014). Promotion of migrant children's epistemic status and authority in early school life. *International Journal of Early Childhood, 47*(1),

5–25. Retrieved from https://doi.org/10.1007/s13158-014-0116-7

Berg, B. L. (2007). *Qualitative research methods for the social sciences.* London, England: Pearson.

Berger, R. (2015). Now I see it, now I don't: Researcher's position and reflexivity in qualitative research. *Qualitative Research,* 15(2), 219–234. Retrieved from https://doi.org/10.1177/1468794112468475

CBS Productions. (1960). *CBS reports: Harvest of shame.* New York, NY: CBS Television.

Carter, C., Reschly, A., Lovelace, M, Appleton, J., & Thompson, D. (2012). Measuring student engagement among elementary students: Pilot of the student engagement instrument-elementary version. *School Psychology Quarterly* 27(2), 61–73.

Casas, R. (2016). *Del otro lado:* Literacy and migration across the U.S.-Mexico border. *Composition Studies,* 44(1), 177–180, 193. Retrieved from http://cupdx.idm.oclc.org/login?url=https://search-proquest-com.cupdx.idm.oclc.org/docview/1791906113?accountid=10248

Cassity, E., & Gow, F. (2005). *Shifting space and cultural place: The transition experiences of African young people in west Sydney schools.* Paper presented at the Australian Association of Educational Research, annual conference, November 27–December 1, Sydney, Australia.

Charmaz, K. (2006). *Constructing grounded theory: A practical guide through qualitative analysis.* Thousand Oaks, CA: Sage.

Chasmar, J. (2017, February 17). Teachers on leave for "Day Without Immigrants" posts reveling in student absences. *The Washington Times*. Retrieved from http://www. washingtontimes.com

Clandinin, D. J., & Connelly, F. M. (2000). *Narrative inquiry: Experience and story in qualitative research*. San Francisco, CA: Jossey-Bass.

Cohen, L., Manion, L., & Morison, K. (2007). *Research methods in education* (6th ed.). London, England: Routledge.

Contreras, F. (2011). *Achieving equity for Latino students: Expanding the pathway to higher education through public policy*. New York: Teachers College Press.

Corbin, J., & Strauss, A. (2008*). Basics of qualitative research: Techniques and procedures for developing grounded theory* (3rd ed.). Thousand Oaks, CA: Sage.

Cranston-Gingras, A., & Paul, J. (2008). Ethics and students with disabilities from migrant farm worker families. *Rural Special Education Quarterly*, 27 (1-2) pps 27–29.

Creswell, J. W. (2013). *Qualitative inquiry and research design: Choosing among five approaches* (3rd ed.). Los Angeles, CA: Sage.

Denzin, N. K., & Lincoln, Y. S. (2008). *Collecting and interpreting qualitative materials*. Thousand Oaks, CA: Sage.

Delgado, D., & Herbst, R.B. (2017). El Campo: Educational attainment and educational well-being for farmworker children. *Education and Urban Society, 50*(4) 328–350.

Devine, D. (2013). 'Value'ing' children differently? Migrant children in education. *Children & Society, 27,* 282–294. https://doi.org/10.1111/chso.12034

DiCicco-Bloom, B., & Crabtree, B. F. (2006). The qualitative research interview. *Medical Education, 40,* 314–321. https://doi.org/10.1111/j.1365-2929.2006.02418.x

Dörnyei, Z. (2007). *Research methods in applied linguistics: Quantitative qualitative, and mixed methodologies.* Oxford, England: Oxford University Press.

Dronkers, J., & Korthals, R. A. (2015). Tracking, schools' entrance requirements and the educational performance of migrant students. ImPRovE Working Paper No. 15/08. Antwerp: Herman Deleeck Centre for Social Policy—University of Antwerp.

Free, J. J., & Križ, K. (2016). "They know there is hope": How migrant educators support migrant students and their families in navigating the public school system. *Children and Youth Services Review, 69,* 184–192.

Free, J., Križ, K., & Konecnik, J. (2014). Harvesting hardships: Educator' views on the challenges of migrant students and their consequences on education. *Children and Youth Services Review, 47,* 187–197.

Glossary of Education Reform (2014. Great School Partnerships. Retrieved from www.edglossary.org/glossary/e/

Goldenberg, B. (2013). White teachers in urban classroom: Embracing non-white students' cultural capital for better teaching and learning. *Urban Education, 49*(1), 111–144. https://doi.org/10.1177/0042085912472510

Gomez, A. (2018, February 26). What the Supreme Court ruling means for DACA and almost 700,000 undocumented immigrants. *USA Today.* Retrieved from https://www.usatoday.com/

Gonzales, R., Terriquez, V., & Ruszczyk, S. (2014). Becoming DACAmented: Assessing the Short-term benefits of Deferred Action for Childhood Arrivals (DACA). *American Behavioral Scientist, 58*(14), 1852–1872. Retrieved from https://doi.org/10.1177/0002764214550288

Green, P. (2003*) The undocumented: Educating the children of migrant workers in America. Bilingual Research Journal, 27*(1), 51–71. https://doi.org/10.1080/15235882.2003.101 62591

Grisham, J., & McCormick, K. (2013). Lessons learned from work with international partners to inform rural practices for early childhood education. *Rural Special Education Quarterly, 32*(1), 3–10.

Gregory, A., Skiba, R. J., & Noguera, P. A. (2010). The achievement gap and the discipline gap: Two sides of the same coin? *Educational Researcher, 39*(1). 59–68. Retrieved from https://doi.org/10.3102/0013189X093576 21?journalCode=edra

Gunderson, G. (2017) *National School Lunch Program: School nutrition a remedy.* Washington, DC: United States Department of Agriculture. Retrieved from https://www.fns.usda.gov/nslp/history_8

Guyll, M., Madon, S., Prieto, L., & Sherr, K.C. (2010). The potential roles of self-fulfilling prophecies, stigma consciousness, and stereotype threat in linking Latino/a ethnicity and educational outcomes. *Journal of Social Issues*, 66, 113–130.

Harper, M., & Cole, P. (2012). Member checking: Can benefits be gained similar to group therapy? *The Qualitative Report, 17*(2). Retrieved from https://nsuworks.nova.edu/tqr/vol17/iss2/1/http://www.nova.edu/ssss/QR/QR17/harper.pdf

Harrison, H. Birks, M., Franklin, R., & Mills, J. (2017). *Case study research: Foundations and methodological orientations. Forum Qualitative Sozialforschung / Forum: Qualitative Social Research, 18*(1), Art. 19. Retrieved from http://nbn-resolving.de/urn:nbn:de:0114-fqs1701195

Hernandez, D.J., Denton, N.A., & Maccartney, S.E. (2008). Children in immigrant families: Looking to America's future. SRCD *Social Policy Report, 22*(3), 3–22

Hooker, S., McHugh, M., & Mathat, A. (2015). Lessons from the local level: *DACA's implementation and impact on education and training success*. Washington, DC: Migration Policy Institute.

Irizarry, S., & Williams, S. (2013). Lending student voice to Latino ELL migrant children's perspectives on learning. *Journal of Latinos and Education, 12*(3), 171–185. Retrieved from https://doi.org/10.1080/15348431.2013.765801

Kossek, E., Meece, D., Barrat, M. E. & Prince, B. E. (2005). U.S. Latino migrant farm workers: Managing acculturative stress and conserving work-family resources. *Work and family: An international research perspective*, 47–70.

Krause, A., Rinne, U., Schüller, S. (2015). Kick it like Özil? Decomposing the native-migrant education gap. *International Migrant Review, 49*, 757–789. https://doi.org/10.1111/imre.12107

Kugler, E. (2018). *How immigrant students strengthen American schools*. Embrace Diverse Schools. Retrieved from https://www.embracediverseschools.com/how-immigrant-students-strengthen-american-schools-2/

Levin, H. M. (2009). The economic payoff to investing in educational justice. *Educational Researcher, 38*(1), 5–19.

Lincoln, Y., & Guba, E. G. (1985). *Naturalistic inquiry*. Newbury Park, CA: Sage.

López, G. R., Scribner, J. D., & Mahitivanichcha, K. (2001). Redefining parental involvement: Lessons from high-performing migrant-impacted schools. *American Educational Research Journal, 38*, 253–288.

Lord, D. (2017). What is DACA and what does today's deadline mean? *Atlanta Journal Constitution*. Retrieved from https://www.ajc.com/news/national/what-daca-and-what-does-today-deadline-mean/atofvpb73cJPtxLN4K17RN/

Lorimer, M. (2016). Cultivating aesthetic and creative expression: An arts-based professional development project for migrant education. *Art Education, Vol. 69*(3), 35–43. Retrieved from http://cupdx.idm.oclc.org/ login?url=https://search-proquest-com.cupdx.idm.oclc. org/docview/1807038609?accountid=10248

Lund, D. E., & Lee, L. (2015). Fostering cultural humility among pre-service teachers: Connecting with children and youth of immigrant families through service-learning. *Canadian Journal of Education, 38*(2), 1-30.

Lundy-Ponce, G. (2010). Migrant students: What we need to know to help them succeed. *Adolescent Literacy.* Retrieved from http://www.adlit.org/article/36286/

Lurie, J. (2015). Just how racist are schoolteachers? *Mother Jones.* Retrieved from http://www.motherjones.com/ kevin-drum/2015/04/teachers-racism-bias-stanford

Mann, B. (2014). *Equity and equality are not equal.* Retrieved from

https://edtrust.org/the-equity-line/ equity-and-equality-are-not-equal/

Martinez, Y. G. (1996). Migrant farmworker students and the educational process: Barriers to high school completion. *High School Journal, 80*(1), 28–38.

Marzano, R. J. (2003). *What works in schools translating research into action* Alexandria, VA: Association for Supervision and Curriculum Development.

Maslow, A. H. (1954). *Motivation and personality.* New York, NY: Harper & Brothers .

McLeod, S. (2017). Maslow's hierarchy of needs. *Simply psychology.* Retrieved from https://www.simplypsychology.org/maslow.html

Merriam, S. B. (2009). *Qualitative research: A guide to design and implementation* (2nd ed.). San Francisco, CA: Jossey-Bass.

Meyers, S. (2012). 'School's not for anybody': Migration as a sponsor of literacy in the USA-Mexico Context. *Power and Education*, 4(2). Retrieved from http://dx.doi.org/10.2304/power.2012.4.2.162

Migration Policy Institute (2014). *Frequently requested statistics on immigrants and immigration in the United States.* Retrieved from http://www.migrationpolicy.org/print/4221#VIMZfKTF_K1

Miles, S. B., & Stipek, D. (2006). Contemporaneous and longitudinal associations between social behavior and literacy achievement in a sample of low-income elementary school children. *Child Development, 77,* 103–117.

Miller, T., Birch, M., & Jessop, J. (2012). *Ethics in qualitative research.* Thousand Oaks, CA: Sage.

Miller, G. (2017). *Connecting migrant students with critical services.* Retrieved from https://www.wested.org/rd_alert_online/migrant-students-education-services/

Murray, C., & Malmgren, K. (2005). Implementing a teacher–student relationship program in a high-poverty urban school: Effects on social, emotional, and academic adjustment and lessons learned. *Journal of School Psychology, 43*(2), 137–152.

Nation's Report Card. (2018). *NAEP reading report card.* Retrieved from https://nces.ed.gov/nationsreportcard/

National Association of Multicultural Education. (2018). *Definitions of multicultural education.* Retrieved from https://www.nameorg.org/definitions_of_ multicultural_e.php

National Center for Farmworker Health, Inc. (2017). *Agricultural worker factsheet.* Retrieved from http://www. ncfh.org/uploads/3/8/6/8/38685499/facts_about_ag_ workers_2017.pdf

Nieto, S. (2002). *Language, culture, and teaching: Critical perspectives for a new century.*

Mahwah, NJ: Erlbaum.

Nordstrom, A., McKibben, K., Baldauf, A., Tachieva, G., & Harding-Pittman. (2012). *Anonymization: The global proliferation of urban sprawl.* Heidelberg, Germany, Kehrer Verlag.

Olwig, K. F., & Valentin, K. (2015). Mobility, education and life trajectories: New and old migratory pathways. *Identities, 22*(3), 247–257. https://doi.org/10.1080/10702 89X.2014.939191

Orth, U., Robins, R. W., & Widaman, K. F. (2012). Life-span development of self-esteem and its effects on important life outcomes. *Journal of Personality and Social Psychology, 102*(6), 1271.

Patton, M. (2015). *Qualitative research and evaluation methods.* Beverly Hills, CA: Sage.

Phipps, R., & Degges-White, S. (2014). A new look at transgenerational trauma transmission: Second-generation Latino immigrant youth. *Journal of Multicultural Counseling and Development*, 42, 174–187.

Pope, N. (2016). The Effects of DACAmentation: The impact of deferred action for childhood arrivals on unauthorized immigrants. *Journal of Public Economics, 143*, 98–114

Quiñones, S., & Marquez Kiyama, J. (2014). *Contra la corriente* (Against the current): The role of Latino fathers in family-school engagement. *School Community Journal, 24*(1). 149–176. Retrieved from https://files.eric.ed.gov/fulltext/EJ1032261.pdf

Rodriguez, A., Abrego, M., & Rubin, R. (2014). Coaching teachers of English language learners. *Reading Horizons, 53*(2).

Rodriguez-Valls, F., & Torres, C. (2014). Partnerships & networks in migrant education: Empowering migrant families to support their children's success, San Francisco 21. ¾. 34–38. Retrieved from https://search-proquest.cupdx.idm.oclc.org/printviewfile?accountid=10248

Romanowski, M. (2013). Meeting the unique needs of the children of migrant farm workers. *The Clearing House, (77)*1, 27–33. Retrieved from http://cupdx.idm.oclc.org/login?url=https://search-proquest-com.cupdx.idm.oclc.org/docview/1698412798?accountid=10248

Russ, E. (2014, Spring). Zero tolerance, zero benefits: The discipline gap in American public K–12 education. *George Mason University, 8*. Retrieved from https://journals.gmu.edu/newvoices/article/view/485

Saldana, J. (2015). *The coding manual for qualitative researchers*. Thousand Oaks, CA: Sage.

Salinas, J. P. (2013). The impact of social capital on the education of migrant children. *Family and Consumer Sciences Journal, 42*(1), 29–39. Retrieved from https://doi.org/10.111/fcsr.12036

Scheiler, A. (2015). *Helping immigrant students to succeed at school-and beyond*. Organization for Economic Co-operation and Development. Retrieved from https://www.oecd.org/education/Helping-immigrant-students-to-succeed-at-school-and-beyond.pdf

Simon, M. K., & Goes, J. (2013). Assumption, limitations, delimitations, and scope of the study. Retrieved from http://dissertationrecipes.com/wp-content/uploads/2011/04/limitationscopedelimitation1.pdf

Solis, J. (2004). *Scholastic demands on intrastate and interstate migrant secondary students. Scholars in the field: The challenges of migrant education*. Charleston, WV: AEL.

Stake, R. (1995). *The art of case study research*. Thousand Oaks, CA: Sage.

Suarez-Orozco, C., & Suarez-Orozco, M. M. (2009). Educating Latino immigrant students in the twenty-first century: Principles for the Obama administration. *Harvard Educational Review, 79,* 327–340.

Sulkowski, M. (2017). Unauthorized immigrant students in the United States: The current state of affairs and the role of public education. *Children and Youth Services Review, 77,* 62–68. Retrieved from https://doi.org/10.16/j.childyouth.2017.04.006

Tavassolie, T., López, C., De Feyter, J., Hartman, S., & Winsler, A. (2018). Migrant preschool children's school readiness and early elementary school performance. *The Journal of Educational Research, 111*(3), 331–344. https://doi.org/10.1080/00220671.2016.1261074

Tellez, K., and Varghese, M. (2013). Teachers as intellectuals and advocates: Professional development for bilingual education teachers. *Theory Into Practice, 52*(2), 128–135

Torrez, J. E. (2014). "Teachers should be like us!": Bridging migrant communities to rural Michigan classrooms. *Multicultural Education, 21*(3), 39–44. Retrieved from http://cupdx.idm.oclc.org/login?url=https://search-proquest-com.cupdx.idm.oclc.org/docview/1648093718?accountid=10248

U.S. Census Bureau (2010). *Urban and rural classification.* Retrieved from https://www.census.gov/library/publications/2013/demo/p20-571.html

U.S. Department of Education. (2002). *The same high standards for migrant students: Holding title 1 schools accountable.* Report No: No-2-2-10. Retrieved from http://www.ed.gov/offices/OESE/OME/pubs.htm

U.S. Department of Education. (2014). *U.S. Departments of Education and Justice release school discipline guidance package to enhance school climate and improve school discipline policies/practices.* Retrieved from https://www.ed.gov/news/press-releases/us-departments-education-and-justice-release-school-discipline-guidance-package-

U.S. Department of Education. (2017). *Office of Migrant Education.* Retrieved from https://www2.ed.gov/about/offices/list/oese/ome/index.html

Vaughn, S., Martinez, L. R., Wanzek, J., Roberts, G., Swanson, E., & Fall, A. (2017). Improving content knowledge and comprehension for English language learners: Findings from a randomized control trial. *Journal of Educational Psychology, 109*(1), 22–34. https://doi.org/10.1037/edu0000069

Vega, D., Lasser, J., & Plotts, C. (2015). Global migration: The need for culturally competent school psychologists. School *Psychology International, 36*(4) 358–374. Retrieved from https://doi.org/10.1177/0143034315587011

Venables, D. R. (2014). *How teachers can turn data into action.* ProQuest Ebook Central, 37–44. Retrieved from http://ebookcentral.proquest.com/lib/concordiaportland/detail.action?docID=1637188.

Vocke, K. S. (2007). *Where do I go from here? Meeting the unique needs of migrant students.* Portsmouth, NH: Heinemann.

Walker, T. (2013). Is America ready to talk about equity in education? *NEAToday.* Retrieved

from http://neatoday.org/2013/05/28/
is-america-ready-to-talk-about-equity-in-education-2/

Whitaker, T. (2013). *What great teachers do differently:
Seventeen things that matter most* (2nd ed.). New York,
NY: Routledge.

Winegard, B., Hasty, C., & Clark, C. (2018). Equalitarianism:
A source of liberal bias. *SSRN Electronic Journal*.
Retrieved from https://www.researchgate.net/
publication/325033477_Equalitarianism_A_Source_of_
Liberal_Bias

Wright, W. (2010. *Teaching English language learners.*
Caslon: Philadelphia, PA.

Yee, J. (2005). Critical anti-racism praxis: The concept of
whiteness implicated. In S. Hick, J. Fook, & R. Pozzuto
(Eds.), *Social work, a critical turn* (pp. 87–104). Toronto,
ON: Thompson.

Yılmaz, F. (2016). Multiculturalism and multicultural
education: A case study of teacher candidates'
perceptions. *Cogent Education*, 3(1) doi:http://dx.doi.org.
cupdx.idm.oclc.org/10.1080/2331186X.2016.117239

Yin, R. K. (2014). *Case study research: Design and methods*
(5th ed.). Thousand Oaks, CA.

About the Author

Dr. Pete Cade has been working in the field of education for nearly three decades, serving the migrant population in rural Southwest Florida. A former migrant student himself, Dr. Cade recognizes the power of an educational system that values all students. Dr. Cade holds a Bachelors Degree in Elementary Education, with a Masters Degree in Educational Leadership. He most recently earned his Doctorate in Teacher Leadership. Dr. Cade has served as a K-6 teacher, Reading Coach, Program Specialist, Principal, and Adjunct Professor. He is currently a Media Specialist where he enjoys sharing his love of literacy with all students.